HRM PRACTICES
IN
INDIAN TOURISM

HRM PRACTICES IN INDIAN TOURISM

Nafees A. Khan
Samar Raza

AKANSHA PUBLISHING HOUSE
NEW DELHI - 110 002 (INDIA)

AKANSHA PUBLISHING HOUSE
4649/21-B, Ansari Road
Daryaganj, New Delhi - 110 002
E-mail: ektabooks@yahoo.com
Phones: 011-23263193, 09435116718
visit us: www.akanshapublishinghouse.com

HRM Practices in Indian Tourism

First Published, 2009

ISBN 978-81-8370-165-5

PRINTED IN INDIA

Published by Akansha Publishing House, New Delhi - 2 and Printed at Capital Offset Press, Delhi.

Contents

	Preface	*vii*
	List of Tables & Figures	*ix*
	Abbreviations	*x*
1.	Introduction	1
2.	Tourism Sector in India: A Profile	30
3.	Human Resource Planning: Theoretical Perspective	61
4.	Recruitment and Selection	81
5.	Training and Development	95
6.	A Case Study of Air Sahara, Jet Airways and ITDC: Analysis and Interpretation	117
7.	Conclusions	156
	Appendices	184
	Bibliography	201
	Index	206

Preface

> "There is a secret pride in every human heart that revolts at tyranny. You may order and drive an individual, but you cannot make him respect you."
>
> —*William Hazlitt*

Effective human resource planning is a process of analyzing an organisation's human resource needs under changing conditions and developing the activities necessary to satisfy these needs.

Human resource planning (HRM) formulates a strategy for the acquisition, utilization, improvement and development of manpower resources. Manpower planning is the system which ensures availability of new personnel developed in terms of quality and quantity and available as and when they are required. Thus, human resource planning refers to establishing job specifications or the qualitative requirement of jobs and determining the number of trained and skilled people required to take up these jobs, as per goals and objectives.

The present study emphasizes as to how forecasting future requirements for human resources, determination of future recruitment and selection needs, linking human resource planning with organisational planning, providing a basis for future management development programmes, ensuring optimum utilisation of human resources presently employed, assessing the surplus and shortage of human resources, control of wage and salary costs, facilitating productivity bargaining would help to improve the organisation's efficiency to achieve its goal by developing strategies that results in optimum utilization of human resources and thereby to help improve productivity at dynamic levels of adequacy.

The study, therefore, examines critically the human resource planning, recruitment and selection, training and development in the tourism sector with special reference to Sahara Airlines, Jet

Airways, India Tourism Development Corporation (ITDC) and Hotel 'The Park'.

The entire information is gathered under seven chapters. First chapter introduces the significance of the study, problems and issues, research gap, scope of the study, objectives, hypotheses, research methodology and review of literature. The second chapter is devoted to the study of profile of tourism sector in India. The third chapter examines theoretical perspectives of manpower planning, while recruitment and selection with special reference to Hotel 'The Park' is dealt in the fourth chapter. The fifth chapter presents training and development in tourism sector. The sixth chapter focuses on case study of Air Sahara, Jet Airways, India Tourism Development Corporation alongwith analysis and interpretation. The last chapter presents summary of findings, conclusions, suggestions and recommendations. Appendices contain vital empirical data.

We wish to place on record my heartfelt gratitude and sincere thanks to Prof. Qamaruddin Khan, Chairman, Department of Commerce, A.M.U. for his unflinching help, advice and inspiration, moral support and encouragement.

We are highly grateful to Prof. Badar Alam Iqbal, Dean, Faculty of Commerce, A.M.U., Aligarh for his assistance, kind interest, advice and generous cooperation.

We are also thankful to Dr. A.Q. Khan, Professor, Department of Commerce for his valuable suggestions, assistance and kind cooperation.

We extend our sincere thanks to all managerial and supervisory staff of ITDC, Air Sahara, Jet Airways and Hotel 'The Park', New Delhi, for their generous cooperation in providing valuable research materials and relevant information.

We are thankful to staff of the Seminar Library, Department of Commerce, A.M.U. Aligarh for their untiring willingness in providing relevant materials as and when required.

We are also thankful to Mr. Hasnain Zafar for typing the script within a short period of time. Finally, we are grateful to our publisher for bringing out this book elegantly.

Dr. Nafees A. Khan
Samar Raza

List of Tables & Figures

TABLES

2.1 Foreign Tourist Arrivals in India (1995-2007) 36

2.2 Domestic Tourist Visits in India (1995-2006) 37

2.3 Foreign Exchange Earnings in India from Tourist (1995-2004) 38

2.4 Plan Outlay from First Five Year Plan to Tenth Five year Plan 47

3.1 Inventory of Human Resources and Future Requirements of Hotel 'The Park', New Delhi 86

5.1 Course-wise Share of Female Candidates 104

6.2 Status of Building Projects of the Institutes of Hotel Management (IHMs) as on 31.03.2004 105

6.1 Financial Performance of India Tourism Development Corporation. 141

6.2 India Tourism Development Corporation Management/ Employees Attitude and Human Resource Planning 146

6.3 AIR SAHARA – Chi-square value 150

6.4 JET AIRWAYS – Chi-square value 151

FIGURES/GRAPHS

3.1 Foreign Tourist Arrivals in India (1995-2004) 71

3.2 Human Resource Flow in a Tourism Organisation 74

Abbreviations

APETT	Asia-Pacific Education & Training Institute in Tourism
CITI	Confederation of Indian Travel Industries
CTE	Central Training Establishment
GSA	General Sales Agent
HRD	Human Resource Development
HRM	Human Resource Management
HRP	Human Resource Planning
IA	Air India
IAL	Indian Airlines Ltd.
IITTM	Indian Institute of Travel and Tourism Management
ILO	International Labour Organization
ITDC	India Tourism Development Corporation
MOU	Memorandum of Understanding
NCHMCT	National Council for Hotel Management and Catering Technology
PSUs	Public Sector Units
TDP	Training and Development Programme
TQM	Total Quality Management
UNEP	United Nations Environment Programme
UN-ESCAP	United Nations Economic & Social Commission for Asia and the Pacific
WIPS	Women in Public Sector
WTO	World Tourism Organization
WTTW	World Travel and Tourism Council
XLRI	Xavier Labour Relations Institute

1

Introduction

> "Man must have the right of choice, even to choose wrong, if he shall ever learn to choose right. The child walks as we unwind the swaddling clothes; the building stands in its full beauty as we remove the scaffolding. Let us beware lest we make goods of scaffolding, lest by making more intricate the wrappings of law, more strong the rods of coercion, man himself remain feeble and imperfect."
>
> **—Josiah C. Wedgwood**

Though the modern era is the age of science and technology computers and automation, man is still the supreme since he invented all these. Of all the resources required for attaining the goals of an enterprise, Human Resource is the most dominant resource. In the organizational setup human resource plays such a vital role that the use of all other resources is dependent upon the Human Resource. The availability, quality, skill, will-to-work, productivity, sincerity, loyalty, etc. make the achievement of the goals of the enterprise. Any kind of deficiency in any of the required attributes in the Human Resource exerts adverse effect on the working of the organization. Enterprises which acquire, develop and manage properly their Human Resource are able to secure their objectives and targets timely and successfully.

In fact, failure of business entities is attributable to a considerably large extent on the lack of Human Resource development, its poor performance, misutilisation and other deficiencies in their workforce. Enlightened enterprises, therefore, pay particular attention to building the stock of Human Resource resource in advance so that workers trained and skilled according to the needs of the organizations are available timely and in sufficient quantity. This calls for the enterprises to engage themselves, as a first priority, in Human Resource Planning for the organization to function smoothly and successfully.

Development of Human Resource is, thus, an activity that involves an action ahead of the time of actual possession of the required Human Resource. Imperative for this purpose to achieve is that there should be systematic planning for the development, training and quality improvement of the Human Resource for the organization. Planning, therefore, emerges as an important pre-requisite in Human Resource Planning, maintenance and utilization.

In fact, planning, is making a decision in advance what is to be done. It is a conceptual plan to follow a pre-determined course of action to achieve the desired results. It is a kind of future picture where events are sketched. It can be defined as a mental process requiring the use of mental faculty, imagination, foresight and sound judgement. It involves seeking solutions to problems and making sound decisions. Plans may be prepared for short time strategy and measure the achievements. Long term plans are prepared to develop the better and new products, services and undertake expansions to keep the interest of the owners.

A well thought-out plan helps make effective use of the available assets and resources for securing the organizational goals. In tourism industry plans need to be prepared to group together the people involved in the industry to achieve the organizational objectives. Planning is also required for coordinating, motivating and controlling of the various activities within the tourism organization. Human Resource Planning for tourism industry also includes forecasting, developing and controlling by which the industry could ensure that it has the right number of people as well as the right kind of people at right places at the right time doing work for which they are economically most useful. Such plans need to be supported by all the members of the organization.[1]

Role of Human Resource Planning

As it deals with the most volatile, sensitive and susceptible human resource, Human Resource Planning occupies a central place in every organizational setup. In the tourism industry there is preponderance of human work force over all other resources. Besides, the workers required for the tourism trade are of variegated nature. Educated, trained, skilled and all other sorts of artisans are engaged in this industry. The necessity for Human Resource Planning for the industry, therefore, is all the more pressing and prominent.

In the present business environment emerging in the wake of liberalization and globalisation, the growing importance of Human Resource Planning for industrial organizations need to be elaborated. Unplanned actions follows uncertainties while planned actions eliminate the uncertainties. Human Resource Planning reduces future uncertainty as related to the acquisition, placement and development of employees for future needs.

It is a sub-system in the total tourism organization planning. It assesses and forecasts future skills requirements, provide control measures to ensures that necessary resources are made available as and when required. It determine recruitment level and optimum training levels, anticipate redundancies and avoid unnecessary dismissals, provide a basis for management development programme, helps organization to identify trouble spots, assist productivity bargaining and deploy Human Resource in new projects.

Human Resource Planning connotes preparation of a schedule, indicating the number of employees of various categories required by the organization over a given period of time. It indicates how many individuals would be selected, trained, promoted, retired over the forthcoming years and to lay down accordingly an estimate of the personnel facilities. It provides information in three dimension – first, estimated Human Resource requirements, second, analysis of the external Human Resource market situation, and third, resulting estimate of Human Resource availability. Human Resource Planning is related to those personnel functions whose purpose is to acquire, develop and maintain a qualified workforce. These functions include recruitment, selection, compensation, career planning, training and development.[2]

Human Resource Planning plays a significant role in ensuring optimum utilization of human resources which can be of great benefit at both national and company unit levels. Human Resource Planning helps in many ways, such as, to forecast compensation cost involved, to develop existing Human Resource to fill the future openings through promotion, to motivate employees, to determine weaknesses of the existing Human Resource so that corrective training could be incorporated. Through adequate and effective Human Resource Planning requisite skills should be developed in existing employees.[3]

Maximum utilization of Human Resource reduces excessive labour turnover and high absenteeism, improves productivity and aids in achieving the objectives of tourism organization. If Human Resource Planning is faultily used, it leads to disruption in the flow of work, high cost of production, lower production and less job satisfaction etc. So, for the success of tourism organization, Human Resource Planning is very important. It helps an individual to improve his skills and utilize capabilities and potential to the utmost. It improves tourism organization's efficiency and productivity. Only through initial Human Resource Planning capable hands are available for promotion in future.

Human Resource Planning provides tourism organization personnel with the necessary qualifications, skills, work experience, knowledge and aptitude for work. It is needed in order to identify areas of surplus or shortage of personnel. In order to meet the needs of expansion programmes of tourism organization Human Resource Planning comes into play its role. To meet the challenges of new and changing technology and new techniques of production, existing employees need to be trained or new employees should be employed. It is necessary due to discharges, marriage, promotions demotions, transfers, retirement, death or incapacitation because of physical or mental ailments, etc.

Human Resource Planning maintains and improves the organizations ability to achieve its goal by developing strategies that will result in optimum contribution of Human Resource. Due to Human Resource Planning, upper level management has a better view of Human Resource dimensions of business decisions, less personnel costs because management can anticipate imbalances before they become unmanageable and expensive, better planning of assignments to develop managers and more time to locate source talent.

Human resource planning also helps maintain and improve the tourism organisation's ability to achieve its goal by developing strategies that will ensure optimum contribution of human resources.

For this purpose, Stainer recommended the following nine strategies for the Human Resource planners.

(a) they should collect, maintain and interpret relevant information regarding human resources;

(b) they should report periodically Human Resource objectives, requirements and existing employment and allied features of Human Resource;

(c) they should develop procedures and techniques to determine the requirements of different types of Human Resource over a period of time from the standpoint of organisation's goals;

(d) they should develop measures of Human Resource utilization as component of forecasts of Human Resource requirements along with independent validation;

(e) they should employ suitable techniques leading to effective allocation of work with a view to improving Human Resource utilization;

(f) they should conduct research to determine factors hampering the contribution of the individuals and groups to the organization with a view to modifying or removing these handicaps;

(g) they should develop and employ methods of economic

assessment of human resources reflecting its features as income-generator and cost and accordingly improving the quality of decisions affecting the Human Resource;

(h) they should evaluate the procurement, promotion and retention of the effective human resources; and

(i) they should analyse the dynamic process of recruitment, promotion and loss to the organization and control these processes with a view to maximizing individual and group performance without involving high cost.

Human resource planning is the responsibility of both the line and the staff manager. The line manager is responsible for estimating Human Resource requirements. For this purpose, he provides the necessary information on the basis of the estimates of the operating levels. The staff manager provides the supplementary information in the form of records and estimates. The staff manager is expected to : (i) report about Human Resource utilization in the present and the past; (i) provide help and advise managers on the assessment of Human Resource utilization and to develop sources of information and techniques for purposes of comparison; (iii) administer the procedure of forecasting or objective setting; (iv) present the overall forecasts of departmental managers; and (v) to advise line managers on forecasting techniques.[4]

Systematic Human Resource Planning is thus a must for every dynamic organization. Despite various pressures, such as political, economic and technological, the challenge has to be met by dynamic management to ensure that the future of the organization remains bright despite changes. For example, the growth of more industries can result in mobility of the personnel and is a source of potential loss of both managerial and other personnel. Fresh people must be ready to fill in such vacancies. If promotion from within is used as far as possible, there is likely to be less agitation from unions. Such a policy can constitute a great motivational force within the organization. This however, entails spotting talent within the organization. Some of the talent probably exists, but in all likelihood some more development is required to fill the higher positions. This is also an important aspect of personnel management. Thus, Human Resource Planning is concerned with anticipating future Human Resource needs at different levels in the organization by visualizing the future and determining how the needed Human Resource can be recruited.

Human Capital

Human Resource is concerned with human beings who are very volatile by nature. All other factors of production like materials, machinery and money are devoid of this characteristics while human force has its own will to act, the material resources are made to act as desired. The development of human resources, which can also be referred to as formation of human capital engages special attention and requires special endeavour of the entrepreneurs. As a matter of fact, the importance of human skills and knowledge and the investment in human capital have become widely recognized as a necessary pre-requisite to non-human capital investment. But the problem in the formation of human capital by way of generation and accumulation of managerial resources is in no way different from the capital formation. So wide is the impact of human capital that a nation's economic development may be limited by the relative shortage of this critical factor or the development may be accelerated significantly by the nation's high capacity to accumulate the human capital. Thus, dependent upon the human resource is the organisation's ability to attain its objectives and develop them in planned way.

Practically, the human resource has at least two concepts. Within corporations and business, human resource most commonly refers to the individuals within the firm as well as that part of the firm's organization which deals with hiring, firing, training and other personal issues. This connotation of human resource has been derived from the various definitions of the term given in political economy and economics, where the human resource was traditionally treated as one of the three factors of production and was called labour.

However, modern analysts emphasize that human beings

are not predictable commodity "resources" with definitions totally controlled by contract, but are creative and social beings that make contributions beyond labour to a society and to civilization. The broad term 'human capital' has evolved to contain the complexity of this term, and in macro-economics the term "firm-specific human capital has evolved to represent the original meaning of the term human resource".

Socialist economies have advocated a central role for human resource or human capital in enterprises and societies. The socialists hold the view that value is primarily created by human activity and, accordingly, human resource justifies a larger claim of profits or relief from these enterprises or societies.

Capitalist economies, however, hold a contrary view. Capitalists contend that human resource is the infrastructural capital or what they call intellectual capital owned and developed by management which provide most value in financial capital terms. This likewise justifies a bargaining position and a general view that human resources are interchangeable.

Developed nations which encourage immigration or "guest workers" are regarded by the governments of developing nations as appropriating human capital that is rightfully part of the developing nation and required to further its growth as a civilization. In the view of developing nations this appropriation is similar to colonial commodity order wherein a colonizing European power would define an arbitrary price for natural resources, extracting of which diminished national natural capital.

The debate regarding "human resources" versus "human capital" thus, in fact, relates to the debate regarding natural resources versus natural capital. Over time the United Nations have come to more generally support the developing nations' point of view, and have requested significant compensating "foreign aid" contributions so that a developing nation losing human capital does not lose the capacity to continue to train new people in trades, professions, and the arts.

An important example of this view is that historical inequities such as African slavery must be compensated by current developed nations, which benefited from stolen "human resources" as they were developing. No doubt, this is an extremely controversial view, but it brings forward the general theme of converting human capital to "human resources" and thus greatly diminishing its value to the host society, i.e. "Africa", as it is put to narrow imitative use as "labour" in the using society.

In the very narrow context of corporate "human resources", there is a contrasting pull to reflect and require workplace diversity that calls for the diversity of a global customer base. Foreign language and culture skills, ingenuity, humor, and careful listening, are examples of traits that such programmes typically require. It would appear that these evidence a general shift to the human capital point of view, and an acknowledgement that human beings do contribute much more to a productive enterprise than "work"; they bring their character, their ethics, their creativity, their social connections, and in some cases even their pets and children, and alter the character of a workplace. The term corporate culture is used to characterize such processes.

The traditional but extremely narrow context of hiring, firing, and job description is considered a 20th century anachronism. Most corporate organizations that compete in the modern global economy have adopted a view of human capital that reflects the modern consensus as above. Some of these, in turn, the term "human resources" as useless.

As the term refers to predictable exploitations of human capital in one context or another, it can still be said to apply to manual labor, mass agriculture, low skill "McJobs" in service industries, military and other work that has clear job descriptions, and which generally do not encourage creative or social contributions.

In general macro-economics treat it this way - as it characterizes no mechanisms to represent choice or ingenuity. So one interpretation is that "firm-specific human capital" as defined in macro-economics is the modern and correct definition of "human resources" and that this is inadequate to represent the contributions of "human resources" in any modern theory of political economy.

Though human resources have been in vogue as part of business and organisations since the first days of agriculture, the modern concept of human resources began in reaction to the efficiency focus of Taylorism in the early 1900s. By 1920, psychologists and employment experts in the United States started the human relations movement, which viewed workers in terms of their psychology and fit with companies, rather than as interchangeable parts. This movement grew throughout the middle of the 20th century, placing emphasis on how leadership, cohesion, and loyalty played important roles in organisational success. Although this view was increasingly challenged by more quantitatively rigorous and less "soft" management techniques in the 1960s and beyond, human resources had gained a permanent role within the firm.

The Society for Human Resource Management (SHRM) is the world's largest association devoted to human resource management. Representing more than 200,000 individual members, the Society's mission is to serve the needs of HR professionals by providing the most essential and comprehensive resources available. As an influential voice, the Society's mission is also to advance the human resource profession to ensure that HR is recognized as an essential partner in developing and executing organizational strategy. Founded in 1948, SHRM currently has more than 550 affiliated chapters and members in more than 100 countries.[5]

G.K. Suri[6] has mentioned that comprehensive Human Resource Planning with a view to secure an optimum utilization of human resources and systematic input in training and development to generate skills at all levels for future manning, a conscious mix of supply within and from outside is practically non-existent. Besides, even now it cannot be claimed that these organizations have been successful in developing such comprehensive Human Resource Planning system as are satisfactory in every respect.

The importance of human factor in the efficient and successful management of industrial enterprises led the managements to think in terms of providing some machinery for managing men. Personnel department came to be recognised as integral part of the managerial setup. The outcome to these developments is the emergence of 'Personnel Management' as a vital part of management studies. Personnel management is productive exploitation of Human resources. This is also termed as 'Human Resource Management' or 'Labour Management' or 'Human Resource Planning". 'Human Resource Management' is a modern term while 'Personnel Management' is traditional term. Scope of 'Human Resource Management' is broad than 'Personnel Management'. Human Resource Management is choosing the proper type of people as and when required. It also takes into account the upgrading in existing people. Human Resource Management starts with Human Resource Planning. Every manager in an organization is a personnel man, dealing with people.[7]

Besides the recognition of the importance of the human factor, some other factors also contributed towards the development of personnel management. To deal with organised labour (i.e., trade unions), to remain in touch with the needs and aspirations of the people at work, and to ensure the observance of a large number of complicated rules framed by the government for the protection of the interests of the workers, some agency was necessary. Since the workers are employed in very large numbers and the work in various departments is of a specialised nature, the management of workers under the factory system of production could not have been carried on by the existing organs of management. A separate department was absolutely essential for copying with this task. The 'personnel department' was created for this purpose.

The proper management of human factor in industry involves careful handling of relationships among the individuals at work. Personnel management, therefore, consists in maintaining these relations on a basis which enables all those engaged in the undertaking to make their best personal contribution to the effective working of the undertaking. The personnel function of management is that part of management which is primarily concerned with human relationships within an organisation. It attempts to ensure the mental and material welfare of the employees so that they work efficiently.

Generally, functions of personnel management can be classified into three main categories, namely, general functions, administrative functions and operative functions. General functions include selection, scientific placement, induction and training, establishing good industrial relations, effective communication, recognise trade union etc.

Administrative functions include planning, organising, directing, staffing, motivating, coordinating etc. Operative functions include procurement (i.e. Human Resource Planning, recruitment, selection and development), development, compensation, integration, maintenance, performance appraisal, etc.

Kautilya provides an excellent disposition on staffing and personnel management embracing job description, qualification for jobs, selection procedures, executive development, incentive systems and performance innovation.[8]

Kautilya provides a systematic treatment of management of human resource as early as 4th century B.C. in his treatise titled *Arthashastra*. As it has been described that there prevailed logical procedures and principles in respect of labour organisation such as *Shreni* or Guild System and co-operative Sector. The wages were paid strictly in terms of quantity and quality of work turned out and punishments were imposed for unnecessarily delaying the work or spoiling it. The Government used to take active interest in the operation of both public and private sector enterprises and provides well-enunciated procedures to regulate employer-employee relationship.[9]

Problems and Issues

The human resource planning has always been the subject of tremendous topical interest. A large number of scholars, authors and professionals have studied the various aspects of Human Resource Planning in India. Dynamic as this activity is, the social, political and economic environment exert their profound influence on the nature of human resource planning. No study can, therefore, fully and finally cover the various aspects of this activity. Despite a plethora of studies conducted in this field there still remain gaps and new issues have cropped up which offer fresh ground to probe this subject in the context of modern development and requirement of human resource.

Some of the glaring problems and issues in Human Resource Planning drawing attention for further research may be elaborated as follows:

- Human resource plans are not balanced with the corporate plans of the enterprise. The methods and techniques used do not fit the objectives, strategies and environment of the particular organization.
- The period of a human resource plan is not appropriate to the needs and circumstances of the specific enterprise. The size and structure of the enterprise as well as the changing aspirations of the people is to be taken into consideration.
- Human resource planning function is not properly organised. A separate cell, section or committee may be constituted within the human resource department to provide adequate focus, and to coordinate the planning efforts at various levels.
- Before starting the human resource planning process the support and commitment of top management is not ensured.

  Moreover, the exercise is not carried out within the limits of a budget. There is no use formulating plans which cannot be implemented due to financial constraints.
- To be successful, human resource planning requires active participation and coordinated efforts on the part of operating executives. Such participation will help to improve understanding of the process and thereby reduce resistance.
- An adequate database is not developed for human resource planning.

- The quantity and quality of human resources is not in tune with the balanced manner. The emphasis is not on filling future vacancies with right people rather than merely matching existing people with existing jobs. Upward mobility of existing staff needs to be considered carefully. Labour turnover is not considered according to length of service rather than merely on aggregate basis.

It is evident from the foregoing enumeration of the gaps in the studies conducted so far that there is still dearth of research studies mainly focusing on the human resource planning in tourism sector in India particularly in the post-liberalization and globalisation regime. The present study is conducted against this backdrop. It includes empirical study on human resource planning, recruitment and selection, training and development, and so on, with special focus on the tourism industry of India. Main hypotheses of this study are::

Ho_1 Unplanned Human Resource development leads to poor productivity in tourism sector in India.

Ho_2 Any expenditure exercise made in planning and development of tourism Human Resource increases the cost of Human Resource and adds less to profitability in tourism sector in India.

Upper management has a better view of the human resources dimensions of business decisions. Personnel costs may be less because management can anticipate imbalances, before they become unmanageable and expensive. More time is provided to locate source talent. Better opportunities exist to include women and minority groups in future growth plans. Better planning of assignments to develop managers can be done.

Human resource planning is practically useful at different levels, as stated by Narayanrao. According to him :

> At the national level, it is generally done by the Government and covers items like population projections, programme of economic development, educational facilities, occupational

distribution, and growth, industrial and geographical mobility of personnel.

At the sector level, it may be done by the Government-Central or State – and may cover Human Resource needs of agricultural, industrial and service sector.

At the industry level, it may cover Human Resource forecast for specific industries, such as engineering, heavy industries, consumer goods industries, public utility industries, etc.

At the level of the individual unit, it may relate to its Human Resource needs for various departments and for various types of personnel.

Manpower planning at the national level is a coordinated effort in a free economy to accelerate the growth and development of industry in a country like India which has been traditionally agricultural. We have already seen that our population is growing very fast, and the pressure on the land is so intensive that unless the country can create more wealth and purchasing power by developing economic pace, it will be difficult for the citizens to enjoy a better and fuller living. In spite of all the planned programmes we have a very large unemployed or under-employed population. It is difficult for a democratic government to leave to problem merely to the adaptation of supply to demand on the basis of market forces.

A proper manpower national planning also helps the people in the placement of jobs in the different areas of the country needing mobility and acquitting the job openings with the aptitude of the workers.

If the national planning is done on a realistic basis and if it is able to provide required information, guidance for training and placement it will certainly help the country to reduce wastage of manpower and to increase productivity and economic growth.

The aim of the national programme is to have a planned policy on the effective utilization of personnel by eliminating waste in respect of material and human resources. It is equally essential for a business enterprise to eliminate waste resources are open to all organisations. The human resources, however, vary from organisation to organization. The effectiveness of an organsiation depends upon its ability like the other factors of production to determine in advance personnel requirements for various jobs in enterprise. It is essential for the management to estimate manpower requirements very carefully not only to meet the current needs but as against the future expansion programmes, labour turnover and the trend of markets governing the supply and demand of both material and human resources.

History has established that an organization which can utilize its manpower resources effectively by motivating them to accomplish company objectives is the organization which forges ahead of others. It is, therefore, becoming increasingly important for an industrial enterprise to plan its Human Resource in such a fashion as it will enable the organization to know the kind of personnel requirement and to locate the sources wherefrom they could be recruited.

In planning the manpower, the management in collaboration with various department heads still determine the personnel requirements for various processes, sections and departments for various categories of staff such as semi-skilled, extra-skilled, unskilled apprentices, clerical and stenography, technical supervisory and management trainees etc. The members of the top management will examine these requirements carefully as against the current demands, future turnover or future expansion programmes and in consultation with the personnel department will co-ordinate its manpower requirements throughout the organization.

In any organization a certain amount of employee turnover always takes place, which may be due to many causes such as physical incapacity, accidents, sickness, retirement, seasonal or cyclical fluctuations in business or death. The community depends upon an enterprise of repute for efficient, courteous and dependable service and today, under complex situations the need for utilizing the skill and experience of the personnel in a systematic manner has become a matter of first importance.

Objectives

(i) To determine future recruitment, selection and training needs.

(ii) To control wage and salary costs.

(iii) To ensure optimum utilisation of human resources presently employed.

(iv) To provide control measures to ensure that necessary human resources are available as and when required.

(v) To link human resource planning with organisational planning.

(vi) To assess the surplus and shortage of human resources.

(vii) To provide a basis for future management development programmes.

(viii) To facilitate productivity bargaining.

(ix) To meet the needs of expansion and diversification programmes.

Salient Features of Present Study

It has been the endeavour of the authors to make an empirical study by analysing and critically examining the relevant statistics collected from primary as well as secondary sources. The primary data were collected through: (a) Questionnaire; (b) Interview; (c) Discussion; and (d) Observation.

Secondary sources include procurement of facts and figures from published and unpublished material. Published sources are reports and official publications of international bodies, central and state and private publications such as journals, periodicals and dailies for different years. Unpublished data include records maintained by the government and private offices, studies undertaken by research institutions, scholars, executives and economists etc. With the help of thorough analysis of these data and their interpretation and examination, fruitful conclusions and findings have been formulated at the end of the study. A case study of Air Sahara, Jet Airways and ITDC has been undertaken in order to make the study more concrete and valuable.

For the purpose of analyzing the collected data, statistical techniques of mean standard deviation and skewness have been used. In order to study the uniformity in the views of various respondents, chi-square test has been applied.

100 employees (not below the rank of Assistant Managers and supervisory levels) in case of Air Sahara and Jet Airways and 125 employees in case of ITDC have been selected. The sampling method has been devised so as to ensure adequate representation for the entire population with regard to Human Resource Planning. The questionnaire consists of 28 statements, out of which 12 relate to ITDC which include questions on human resource planning, recruitment and selection, training and development and so on. The objective of framing questionnaire is as to elicit information relating to forecasting future requirements for human resources, determination of future recruitment and selection needs, linking human resource planning with organisational planning, providing a basis for future management development programmes, ensuring optimum utilisation of human resources presently employed, assessing the surplus and shortage of human resources, control of wage and salary costs, facilitating productivity bargaining and so on.

Pilot survey has been undertaken for pre-testing the questionnaire. Questionnaire has been edited in the light of the results of the pilot survey. The questionnaire includes 28 statements relating to assessment regularly of the surplus and shortage of human resources, determination of levels of future recruitment and selection needs, determination of future training and management development needs, controlling of wage and salary costs, to ensure optimum utilization of human resources employed, to provide a basis for future management development programmes, to make efforts to meet the needs of expansion and diversification programmes, full development of human resource information system, status of growth of productivity, unplanned Human Resource development leads to poor productivity, poor Human Resource Planning leads to unencouraging profitability and any expenditure made in planning and development of Human Resource increases the cost of

Human Resource and adds less to profitability, to identify and utilize the potential of the employees, whether human resource information system has been fully developed in the organization, employees feel that proper Human Resource national planning helps the people in the placement of jobs in the different areas of the country, employees feel that in spite of all the planned programmes still there is a very large unemployed or underemployed population and so on.

II

The human resource planning has always been the subject of tremendous importance to every organization using human force to achieve its objectives. In fact, the quality of the organization, to a large extent, is dependent on the overall quality of the people it acquires and utilises. Human resource planning serves as the management tool to decide on the quality and quantity of the people required for the organization. It becomes a pre-requisite to ensure that the right people are available for the right job at the right time. In view of its vital importance to the organisations, a large number of scholars, authors and professionals have focused their attention and studied the various aspects of human resource planning in India.

Dessler, Garry in his book entitled, *Human Resource Management* (2004) provides a most complete and applied review of human resource management concepts, techniques, and practices in a highly readable and understandable form. In his book he presents strategic role of human resource in achieving high performance within each organisation.

Tripathi, P.C. in his book entitled *Human Resource Planning* (2005) deals with the routine functions of personnel manager and describes in detail Human Resource Planning techniques such as quality circles, quality of work life, training, counselling, participation, welfare, grievances mechanism-for workers; and performance appraisal, potential appraisal, training and development, role analysis for managers.

Kandula, Srinivas R. in his book entitled *Strategic Human*

Resource Planning (2004) states that Human Resource Planning must strive to bring synergy between theory and practice and talks in tangible terms on how Human Resource Planning can benefit the organisations and employees.

Aswathappa, K. in his book entitled *Human Resource and Personnel Management – Text and Cases* (2004) states that Indian industry is working up to the challenges thrown in by market economy. To survive in this highly competitive scenario, managers are being pressured to improve quality, increase productivity, cut down waste and eliminate inefficiency. The collective efforts of the employer and employee assume relevance in this context and this is where human resource management can play a crucial role. In this book sincere attempt has been made towards the understanding of human resource in its proper perspective.

Monappa, Arun and Saiyadain, Mirza in their book entitled, *Personnel Management* (2002) cover some of the changes that are taking place in existing or traditional personnel functions/ practices. These changes are due to the increased importance being given to functions, such as selection or training, by organizations wanting to identify and utilize human resources as efficiently as possible.

Sabhanayakam, S. in his book entitled, *Human Resources: Development and Utilization (with special reference to India)* (2002) analyses varied theories of the economists on the subject 'Development and Utilization of Human Resources' (with special reference to India and Tamil Nadu). The demographic changes, predominance of rural population and the backwardness and indifference of the female population in developmental efforts are highlighted in a logical and scientific way.

Kumar, Ashok in his book entitled *Human Resource Management Challenge of Change* (2004) highlights the major challenge confronting modern management thought and practice and concludes that a viable Human Resource Planning strategy is essential to cope with the increasing demand for super-skilled personnel by rapidly growing business and commerce, trade and industry, corporate and multinational entities, and the burgeoning public sector and government systems.

Sarma, A.M. in *Personnel and Human Resource Management* (2003) stresses that there is an urgent need to understand the constant changes in the environmental factors and human resources and to find proper solutions to the various problems arising therefrom. The responsibility to find out the solutions to these problems lies with every manager who has to deal with different changes effectively through educational and development programmes. The objective of this book is to enhance the understanding of these problems with a view to promoting the effective management of human resources in changing organisational settings.

Bhasin, M.L. in his book entitled *Human Resources Management: The Case Studies* (2004) focuses upon problems and policies of managing people in organisations. Its objective is to assist the practicing or potential managers in developing the awareness, knowledge and skills needed to solve human problems and to make appropriate organisational decisions.

Mamoria, C.B. and Gankar, S.V. in their book entitled *Personnel Management* (2002) present a comprehensive discussion of the elements that go to make up the management of human resources. Human beings are a resource to an organisation. Like any other material on economic resources they represent an investment whose development and utilisation require managing.

Flippo, Edwin B. in his book entitled *Personnel Management* (2002) has summarized that personnel management is the planning, organizing, directing, and controlling of the procurement, development, compensation, integration, maintenance and separation of human resources, to the end that individual, organizational, and societal objectives are accomplished.

Yoder, Dale and Staudohar, Paul D. in their book entitled *Personnel Management and Industrial Relations* (2002) have stated that examination of the major functional areas of personnel management and industrial relations such as organisation, recruitment, selection, appraisal, training and development, wage and salary administration, and labour relations, etc. is significant. The systems approach is used to integrate materials and show the relationships among functional areas.

Rudrabasavaraj, M.N. in his book entitled, *Dynamic Personnel Administration – Management of Human Resources* (2002) discusses the nature and evolution and develops certain concepts, theories, and principles in the field of personnel administration. He then sets forth the policies, programmes and procedures of the various operative and advisory functions, dealing in detail the personnel tools and techniques utilised in India and U.S.A. He points out some of the trends in the field of personnel administration and the kind of challenge facing the personnel executives. Both philosophical concepts and practical ideas are presented.

Pettman, Barrie O. and Tavernier, Gerard in their book entitled *Human Resource Planning Workbook* (1998) have explained the objectives of Human Resource Planning, designing a manpower information system, manpower requirements, analysis of internal and external manpower supply, improving manpower utilization, improvement of manpower policies within the company, analysis and control of training, and controlling manpower costs etc.

Ghosh, P. in his book entitled *Personnel Administration in India* (2002) has stated that the behavioural science approach is gradually gaining ground in the art of handling men in India. Define the philosophy and goals of the Indian working class vis-à-vis the leadership of the professional managers in motivating a work-force which till now has not adapted itself to an industrial climate. Drawn freely upon the theories prevalent in the industrially advanced countries of the world and examined their applications on the problems of personnel administration in the Indian context.

Davar, Rustom S. in his book entitled *Personnel Management and Industrial Relations in India* (2002) states that personnel function is presented in the conceptual focus of the manager's job, and thereafter is concerned with Human Resource Planning, recruitment and selection, training and development facilities including suitable promotions and transfers, performance appraisals. And then indicates how personnel productivity can be enhanced through an adequate system of motivation and suggestions are made for better industrial relations.

Hax, Arnoldo C. in his book entitled *Planning Strategies that Work* (2002) has endeavoured to provide practicing managers with a systematic range of ideas and applications in the ever-important area of planning for the future in organizations'.

Walley, B.H. in his book entitled *Management Services Handbook* (2001) discusses the role of management services, diagnosis and appraisal techniques, measurement techniques, planning, strategy formulation and general management methods, control of performance, motivation and communication, aids to decision-making and profit improvement.

Finble, Robert B. and Jones, William S. in their book entitled *Assessing Corporate Talent – A Key to Managerial Human Resource Planning* (2001) describe an assessment process that has been in use in one company for over seven years. Primary attention is devoted to explaining how the program uses present day assessment technology in ways that help the management of the organization understand and build confidence in the results and how these results affect Human Resource Planning decisions. It points to the value of using a wide variety of testing and assessment techniques and of having psychologists and managers work jointly on the assessment process itself. It is not a survey of testing theory or a resource book of available technique.

Chopra, Rakesh K. in his book entitled *Management of Human Resources* (2002) has made an attempt to present a comprehensive analysis of principles, tools, concepts and techniques which is only helpful to the practicing managers and not to others.

Gupta, C.B. in his book entitled *Human Resource Management* (2004) has mentioned that human resource management is a set of policies, practices and programmes designed to maximize both personnel and organizational goals. It is the process of binding people and organizations together that the objectives of each are achieved. It does not consider the productivity aspect.

According to National Institute of Personnel Management of India, "personnel management is that part of management concerned with people at work and with their relationships within the organization. It seeks to bring together men and women who make up an enterprise, enabling each to make his own best contribution to its success both as an individual and as a member of a working group". It does not consider the aspect of organisational culture and effectiveness.

As opined by the National Committee on Tourism, Planning Commission, Government of India, the present system of tourism training programme suffers from several weaknesses both in qualitative and quantitative dimensions. Yet, those trained under these schemes are better than those having no education and training for they can comparatively add to more productivity in the tourism sector.

Asia Pacific and Training Institutes in Tourism (APETIT), United Nations Environment Programme (UNEP), International Labour Organisation (ILO), World Tourism Organisation (WTO) and the World Travel and Tourism Council (WTTC) etc., concerned with human resource planning to achieve productivity at maximum level in tourism sector have not made indepth country-specific study pertaining to Human Resource Planning in tourism sector in India, particularly after the implementation of the policy of economic liberalization.

Agarwal, Nair and Banerjee in the book entitled *Human Resource Management* (2004) has mentioned that the purpose of this book is to assimilate new insights from human resource management and behavioural sciences into established concepts. In order to make this more interesting, the author has utilized the concept of formulating the plan to divide the book contents into small units. Attempts have been made to approach empirically to the practical problems of human resource management.

Bhatnagar, K.P. in his book entitled *Transport in Modern India* (2003) has shown the role and significance of Civil aviation in India and abroad. He has examined critically the growth and development of various mode of transport in India and its effect on the economy of the country.

Prasad, L.M. in his book entitled *Human Resource Management* (2003) has tried to place proper emphasis on the human resources of the organization. It presents the most recent developments in the field and tries to relate how these developments are relevant to Indian Companies. It incorporates the human resource management practices being followed by the leading Indian Companies in their respective fields. It has failed to focus on Human Resource Planning in tourism sector.

Gupta, Shishi K. and Joshi, Rosy in their book entitled *Human Resource Management* (2004) have laid emphasis only on the effectiveness of Management of Human Resources.

Tripathi, P.C. in his work *Personnel Management and Industrial Relations* (2005) has stated that there has been an increase in prestige and power of Personnel Manager in India in comparison to past practice when organizations used their personnel departments as a sort of dumping ground for executive misfits. The enterprises have now started putting their personnel management in the hands of powerful senior executives.

Reddy, Sumati in her edited book entitled *E-Learning and Technology: New Opportunities in Training and Development* (2003) has highlighted how distance training and education helps organizations meet the challenge of organizational change their personnel practices reach competitive standards, and achieve organizational goals. Distance and online training is considered as an investment in people which helps in meeting pre-determined objectives.

Managerial Effectiveness, Vol. II, Concepts and Cases edited by Prasad, V.R.K. (2004) states that effective management is right thinking and right acting and the effective manager has to be a competent theorist and practitioner. Managerial effectiveness is beyond enhancing managerial skills and behavioural competencies.

Raina, A.K. and S.K. Agrawal, in their book entitled, *The Essence of Tourism Development (Dynamics, Philosophy and Strategies)* (2004) present a comprehensive view and analytical understanding to form a strategy for tourism promotion, marketing with impact assessment on the economy.

Matiram in his book entitled *International Tourism – Socio-Economic Perspectives* (2003) focuses on growth and trend of international tourism, tourism motivation and infrastructure, tourism policy and planning and impact assessment, etc.

Sajnani, Manohar in his book entitled, *Indian Tourism Business – A Legal Perspective* (2003) presents principles and practices of tourism business in India in general and with particular emphasis on its legal and regulatory aspects.

Narasaiah, M.L. in his book entitled, *Globalization and Sustainable Tourism Development* (2004) stresses on internationally coordinated efforts to make tourism environmentally and socially sustainable.

Sharma, K.K. in his book entitled, *Tourism and Development* (2005) focuses on nature based tourism and ecotourism trend and issues in tourism industry management, tourist attraction, sustainable tourism, and globalization. He also dwells upon the economic impacts of tourism, tourism and leisure, individual consumption of tourism, tourism industry, tourism and entrepreneurship, tourism employment and labour markets, etc.

Malhotra, R.K. in his book entitled *Human Resource Issues in Hotel Industry* (2002) focuses on importance of human resources, planning and development for human resource, education and training for human resource in hotel industry, review of occupations in the hotel industry, role of trade unions, using information on human resources in hospitality industry, human resource strategy in hotel management, sociology and working in the hotel industry and corporate performance appraisal etc.

Selvam, M. in his book entitled, *Tourism Industry in India: A Study of Its Growth and Its Developmental Needs* (2002) stresses on economics of tourism, growth of tourism, tourism infrastructure – attractions, accommodation, transportation, travel agents and tourism development, tourist guides, tourism publicity and promotion, satisfaction index, government policy and tourism, etc.

Bhatia, A.K. in his book entitled *International Tourism – Fundamentals and Practices* (1998) sets out the global aspect of tourist industry in its various manifestations. The contents cover the nature, structure, and organization of the global tourist industry and its impact on various economic, social and cultural aspects of nations.

Singh, Ratandeep in his book entitled *Infrastructure of Tourism in India* (1998) explains the state of tourism industry in India, planned approach to tourism development, tourism infrastructure and manpower development, tourism marketing strategies, promoting India, hospitality industry in Asia and regional tourism potential etc.

W.G. Scott, Clothier, R.C. and Spriegel, W.R. in their book entitled, *Personnel Management – Principles, Practices and Point of View* (2000) define the Personnel Management as "that branch of management which is responsible on a staff basis for concentrating on those aspects of relationship of management to employees and employees to employees and with the development of the individual and the group the objective is to attain maximum individual development, desirable working relationship between employers and employees and employees and employees, and effective moulding of human resources as contrasted with physical resources". They elaborate on it and deal with various aspects of personnel management.

Prasad, Lallan and Banerjee, A.M. in their book entitled, *Management of Human Resources* (2003) have stressed that manpower is a primary resource without which other resources like money, material etc. cannot be put to use. In their view even a fully automatic unit such as unmanned satellite requires manpower to execute it and plan further improvements/activities. That is why man learnt the use of manpower much before he learnt to use other resources.

Devi, Laxmi in her book entitled, *Human Resource Management* (2002) analysed that human resource is an important corporate asset and overall performance of companies depends upon the way it is put to use. In order to realize company objectives, it is essential to have a manpower plan. Human Resource Planning or Human Resource Planning is essentially the process of getting right number of qualified people into the right job at the right time. It is a system of matching the supply of people (existing employees and those to be hired or searched for) with the openings the organization expects over a given time frame. She concludes that Human Resource Planning, thus, involves two things: (i) employment planning and (ii) programme planning

Patnayak, Biswajeet in his book entitled *Human Resource Management* (2004) has focused on chapters like HRM for Corporate Excellence, Knowledge Creation and Management and OD but has not mentioned HRP in Tourism Industry in India.

Basu, C.R. in his book entitled, *Management of Human Resource* (2003) "to bring out the best in man is the essence of Human Resource Planning".

Narayan, B. in his book *Human Resource Practices in Organisations* (2002) has remarked that "the Human Resource Planning is a continuous process and can be achieved by organizing the organizational process in a scientific method, which can create organizational climate for development, motivate human resource to do a job, can give feeling of a team and can develop commitment in the people".

Mathur, Navin in his paper "Manpower Management for Improving Productivity in Public Enterprises", in *International Journal of Management and Tourism,* Vol. 1, No. 3, January-March, 1993, pp. 373-381, has suggested measures to improve Manpower Management which is one of the ways to increase productivity and efficiency of Indian Public Enterprises. However, the Paper does not base its study on survey and primary data.

The present authors have consulted a number of national and international journals an Tourism and HRD.

They have also searched relevant ongoing projects on internet. In addition a number of M.Phil. dissertations and Ph.D. theses on Human Resource Management and Human Resource Planning were also consulted.

REFERENCES

1. http://www.buzzle.com/editorials/9-12-2004-59200.asp.
2. Sharma, A.M. (2003), *Personnel and Human Resource Management*, Himalaya Publishing House, Mumbai, pp. 44-46.
3. Davar, Rustom S. (1980), *Personnel Management and Industrial Relations in India*, Vikas Publishing House Pvt. Ltd., New Delhi, pp. 63-64.
4. Mamoria, C.B. and Gankar, S.V. (2002), *Personnel Management – Text and Cases*, Himalaya Publishing House, Mumbai, pp. 156-158.
5. http://en.wikipedia.org/wiki/Human resources.
6. Suri, G.K. (1974), 'Human Resource Practices in Indian Industry,' *Indian Management*, Vol. 13, No. 8.
7. http://en.wikipedia.org/wiki/Human resources.
8. Sharma, M.K. (1977), 'Kautilya and Management,' *Indian Management*, July, p. 31.
9. *Kautilya Arthashastra* (Translated by Shamasastry, R.) (1956), Shri Raghuveer Printing Press, Mysore, pp. 30-34.

2

Tourism Sector in India: A Profile

> "One man can completely change the character of a country, and the industry of its people, by dropping a single seed in fertile soil."
>
> **—John C. Gifford**

In fact, considerably commendable work has been done by a large number of scholars and professional in the field of HR. These works make fairly wide coverage of various aspects concerning the human resource. Much, however, has been left out for fresh research on human resource planning particularly in the context of tourism sector of India. This study dwells upon this sector and traces the Human Resource Planning practices prevalent in the tourism industry. But before embarking upon the probe into these Human Resource Planning practice in the Indian tourism sector, it is considered necessary to provide an insight into the present status of the tourism sector. The present chapter accordingly, is devoted to present a profile of the tourism sector in the pre- and post-globalisation era.

In technical terms tourism comprises activities of persons travelling to and staying in places outside their usual environment for leisure, business and other purposes for not more than one year at a stretch. A person, however, becomes a tourist if he stays for a minimum of 24 hours at a place and incurs expenditure there. Increase in prosperity alongwith modes of faster travel and other infrastructural developments have contributed to growth of tourism at a fast rate and more and more people are having access to paid holidays. Tourism today is the world's largest export industry. Tourism is also a major contributor to foreign exchange earnings of several developing and even developed countries.[1]

The Government of India declared tourism as an industry in 1986. The tourism industry has since been officially defined to include the accommodation sector, travel related services like travel agents, tour operators, reservation systems, amusement parks, special health units and conventions organizers. Tourism has emerged as the biggest industry of the future. The growth of world tourism was slow in the first part of the last century, rapid in the later part and phenomenal since 1980s.[2]

Significance of Tourism Sector

Today, tourism has acquired the status of a major industry, playing a decisive role in the world economy. In fact, travel and tourism taken together constitute the largest industry in terms of turnover and employment. Tourism has played a very important role in the history and development of India. India has always been a tourist's delight and traveller's destination.[3]

Travel and tourism in India is an integral part of Indian tradition and culture. In the olden days, travel was primarily for pilgrimage. People also travelled to participate in *melas,* fairs and festivals in different parts of the country. In such a background developed a cultural tradition where 'Atithi Devo Bhava' (the guest is God) and 'vasudhaiva Kutumbakam' (the world is one family) became bywords of Indian social behaviour. From ancient time, the rulers in different parts of India built luxurious palaces, enchanting gardens, marvelous temples, grand forts, tombs and memorials giving expression to the depth of one's feelings and sentiments. These remain today as testimony to the rich cultural heritage of this land, and as examples of exquisite craftsmanship of the people of the ages gone past. The variety of such creation is exciting. The grandeur of many of these is quite breathtaking. The beauty of India's cultural heritage and the richness of the nature's endownments make India a tourist's paradise. The enthusiasm to visit these places and explore new ones continues.

Tourism is also seen as an important instrument for national integration and international understanding. People of different origin, religion and nations interact with each other through the media of tourism. This develops between them an understanding and tolerance of each other and contributes to fostering world brotherhood.

In India tourism captured the attention of central government soon after the country achieved Independence in 1947. Even in the initial years of economic planning, the importance of creating the infrastructure was recognized. The five star hotel Ashok, the pride of the Government in those days, came up in the 1950s. The India Tourism Development Corporation (ITDC) was also set up as an umbrella organization to develop tourism infrastructure at a time when private initiative in these areas was not so abundant.[4]

In India organized tourism began in the 50s with the genesis of planned development. It contributes to national integration and promotion of an environment of social and cultural lives.[5] Today, tourism is as much a part of socio-economic development as any other activity.

Several states of India have recognized tourism as an industry in the last decade and thus entitling the tourism industry to several incentives including subsidies and prioritization in the grant of loans. At the very start of economic reforms in 1991 tourism was declared a priority sector for foreign investment. To ensure a broad spread of the gains from tourism several tourist circuits and destinations have been identified for development. The state government of Kerala, Tamil Nadu, Orissa, Maharashtra and the Union territory administration of Daman and Diu have identified destination to be developed under the Special Tourism Area Authority. Here, investors on a wide range of facilities will get special incentives on the lines of what are available of the export processing zones. The places are Bekal beach in Kerala, Puri-Konark in Orissa, Sindhudurg in Maharashtra, Muttakadu Mamallapuram in Tamil Nadu and Diu beach.[6]

There would be benefits for almost everybody in an upswing of Indian tourism. In this beneficial horizon, gains would accrue among others to business, trade, shopping, lodging and catering, financial services, the transport industry, the arts and crafts, and picturesque regions howsoever remote. Tourism has tremendous employment potential, as it is a highly labour intensive industry. Even in a lean year like 1994-95, the Indian tourism industry generated over one million jobs. There are also invisible benefits flowing from a spurt in domestic tourism. By generating better understanding among people from various regions, it is perhaps the most effective instrument for national integration. What is also not realized is that tourism, apart from earning foreign exchange can bring about integrated community development and thereby help improve the quality of life of the people. In many ways tourism can be a self-sustaining business, once a modicum of infrastructure is provided. The important task is to get tourism accepted as an instrument of development and national integration. For this it is necessary to create an awareness of India's charms as a tourist paradise, simultaneously address the important aspect of toning up infrastructure, and then get down to marketing the product in a pragmatic and result-oriented manner.[7]

Tourism has significant linkage with several other sectors like agriculture, horticulture, poultry, handicrafts, construction etc. Several items of tourist expenditure induce a chain of transactions in these sectors and each such transaction calls for the supply of some kind of goods and services. Further, those directly or indirectly employed following the development of tourism may also demand more goods and services as a result of such employment than what they would have demanded otherwise. The additional consumption demand, thus emanating from tourist expenditure will not only induce more employment, but also generate a further multiplier effect through a successive chain of transactions.[8]

Aviation has become the principal means of travel. Domestic air services took tourists to destinations far beyond the Taj and more foreign carriers choose India for their services to the Far

East. Soon hotels too became profitable ventures with the deluxe segment attracting entrepreneurs. A new crop of five stars appeared on the horizon. Again, it was an Ashok in Bangalore, south India's first five star hotel. Apart from hotels there was major growth in the travel agency sector. Joining the list headed by Thomas Cook, Cox and Kings and American Express were Sita, Orient Express, TCI, Ind Travels, Mercury, SOTC, Ambassador Tours, to mention only a few. The emergence of trade bodies was not far behind. FHRAI (Federation of Hotels and Restaurants Association) and TAAI (Travel Agents Association of India) are among the oldest while IATO, (India Association of Tour Operators) and Hotel Association of India are among the later entrants. Adventure tour operators, domestic tour operators and tourist transport operators have their own bodies.[9]

Economic Aspect

Tourism is a means of increasing the level of economic activity of the host nation through sale of products and services to the travellers. Travel to an area provides a basis for developing tourism as an export industry. These economic inputs are in terms of revenue and employment. The amount of tourism expenditure that remains in the area provides a source of income to local residents and is considered as the direct effect of visitors expenditure. The secondary effect comes as the money paid by the visitors to the business is utilized to pay for supplies, wages of workers and other items used for the benefit of the visitors.

Tourism multiplier is estimated on the basis of sales and output employment or payroll or other variables. As the number of visitors making purchases increases, demand for products and services produced in the area is also increased which directly or indirectly creates employment opportunities for the residents. In our country we have sufficient resources to increase production to meet the higher demand and thus, the full amount of tourist expenditure will remain in the country. The visitors expenditure in the country should be considered as an export, since the products and services are sold to the people who come from outside the area. Thus tourism development provides an external source of income to our country's economy and its development.

Employment Aspect

The social aspect of tourism development in our country is related to the creation of new job opportunities and influx of new income to the concerned area. As such, a broad tourism development programme should incorporate measures for educational and training facilities for the local residents. It has come to be realised now that the hotels' cultural shock on the community is slowly wearing off and its benefits are outweighing the negative aspects. Increase in income high standard of living, a sense of increased self-worth and accomplishment, social contact with the fellow employees and tourists are some of the benefits of tourism development.

Additional revenue thus generated also raises the general level of income and employment in the country and changes the quality of life for the residents.

Tourism Publicity

Tourism publicity developed under the pressure of growth of international travel and competition in the globalised environment. The information has to be supplied to the ever increasing number of tourists about the country, its tourism destination, tourism products, etc. New items of interest to travel industry such as comfortable, cheap and world class transport facilities, new tourist resorts, various sorts of tourism potential of the country were highlighted to tourism through multimedia approach. Besides the print media, electronic media is also extensively used now. All India Radio, Doordarshan are giving much impetus in this regard. Several tourist films are produced by different state tourism corporations. Lectures, seminars and workshops are arranged to highlight the importance of tourism as an industry which earns foreign exchange. Advertisements in various magazines and daily newspapers are issued depending on their budget. Newspapers bring out supplements. The publicity journal is more representative than all other forms of print material, though it is expensive and limited in its circulation.

Tourist Arrivals in India and Foreign Exchange Earnings from Tourism

With the development and expansion of facilities, the tourism industry of India has got a big boost. Hospitality of people coupled with cheap cost of lodge and board, travel and transport have further made India a preferred destination for tourists. The number of tourists visiting India is continuously rising. Table 2.1 presents the statistics of the arrivals of foreign tourists during the decade 1995-2004. Also the percentage increase/decrease in tourist arrivals over the previous year is given in the table.

TABLE 2.1

Foreign Tourist Arrivals in India (1996-2007)

Year	*Foreign Tourist Arrivals*	*Percentage Change*
1996	22,87,860	7.7
1997	23,74,094	3.8
1998	23,58,629	-0.7
1999	24,81,918	5.2
2000	26,49,378	6.7
2001	25,37,282	-4.2
2002	23,84,364	-6.0
2003	27,26,214	14.3
2004	34,57,477	26.8
2005	39,18,610	13.3
2006	44,29,915 (P)	13.0

Source: Annual Report (2006-2007), India Tourism, Government of India, New Delhi, p. 98.

(P) = Provisional

Obviously, the data in Table 2.1 states that there has been a healthy growth of 23.5 per cent in the tourist arrivals from other countries during the decade under study.

The growth however, has been fluctuating over the period

1996-2006. There has been negative growth in 1998 when the foreign tourist arrivals fell by 0.7 per cent over the previous year. The decrease is attributable to violence in the Kashmir valley and the Kargil war. Likewise the number of foreign visitors dropped in the years 2001 and 2002 consecutively by 4.2 and 6.0 per cent respectively. This slump in the arrivals of foreign tourists had been caused due to panic effect world over in the aftermath of 11 Sept. 2001 episode in USA. The war against terrorism was launched and as a consequence world tourism suffered a setback. Soon the recovery started, confidence restored and the tourism activity got revived. The years 2003 saw a positive growth in foreign tourists arrivals of 14.3 per cent which further rose to 23.5 per cent in the year 2004. During the year 2006, the foreign tourists arrival have been 4429915 approximately, registering a growth of 13.0 percent in comparison to the previous year.

TABLE 2.2

Domestic Tourist Visits in India (1995-2006)

Year	*Domestic Tourist Visits*	*Percentage Change*
1995	13,66,48,600	—
1996	14,01,19,672	2.5
1997	15,98,71,008	14.1
1998	16,81,96,000	5.2
1999	17,60,82,442	4.7
2000	19,45,72,313	10.5
2001	22,87,30,890	14.9
2002	25,10,00,000	9.7
2003	27,13,45,504	8.1
2004	31,15,54,408	14.8
2006	44,29,91,500	42.18

Source: Annual Report (2006-2007), Ministry of Tourism, Government of India, New Delhi, p. 166.

On the domestic front there has been tremendous growth of tourists as would appear from Table 2.2. The data on domestic tourists in Table 2.2 reflect that there has been an approximately three fold increase over the period 1995 to 2004. The growth pattern, however, is not steady and fluctuations in growth rate appear till the year 2000. In the subsequent years the number of domestic tourists has been consistently on rise with the exception of 2001 and 2002 when terrorism had its profound impact on tourism globally.

With the arrival of foreign tourists there comes the invisible foreign exchange. Table 2.3 presents the data relating to foreign exchange earnings through the foreign visitors during the decade 1995-2004.

TABLE 2.3

Foreign Exchange Earnings in India from Tourism (1995-2006)

Year	*Foreign Exchange Earnings (Rs. in crores)*	*Percentage Change*
1995	8,430	—
1996	10,046	19.2
1997	10,511	4.6
1998	12,150	15.6
1999	12,951	6.6
2000	14,238	9.9
2001	14,344	0.7
2002	14,195	-1.0
2003	16,429	15.7
2004	21,828	31.5
2005	25,172	16.5
2006	29,604(P)	17.6

Source: Annual Report (2006-2007), Ministry of Tourism, Government of India, New Delhi, p. 166.

(P) = Provisional.

It is obvious from the Table 2.3 that the foreign exchange brought in India by the foreign visitor rose from Rs. 8,430 crores in 1995 to Rs. 21,828 crores in 2004. The growth works out 32.9 per cent in 2004 over 2003. There have been positive growth in foreign exchange earnings though in fluctuating order during the decade, except in the year 2002 when the rate of growth is negative at –1.0 per cent. The decline in foreign exchange earnings in 2002 is attributable to 11 Sept. terrorist attack in USA which shook the security confidence of the tourists world over. During the year 2006 the estimated foreign exchange earning were Rs. 29603.56 crore as compared to Rs. 25172.28 crore during the same period of 2005.

Social Perspective

Consequent upon the publicity measures taken by the Government to popularize the tourism and create an awareness about tourism potential of India, there has come about a prominent change in the attitude of the domestic and foreign tourists. An urge has emerged in them to visit the various places in India with rich tourism heritage of its glorious history. The new attitude has changed the traditional view of tourism for pilgrimage to modern view of tourism for pleasure and utilizing leisure and at the same time learning through each other.

As per traditional notion, tourism was considered as a luxury and meant only for rich who could afford travel. Now it is held to be normal part of life style. The concept of pleasure travel has completely changed. Foreign travel during pre-Independence was for the rich. Today the travellers comes from wider social, cultural, religious background with varied tastes. More people are now going abroad to explore the world and to know about people and places. Advanced modern technology has brought about a completely new dimension to modern tourism. Tourism is essentially a pleasure activity in which one's hard earned money is spent. Transport, locales and accommodation are the basic components of tourism. Historic and cultural factors added to these components attract the tourists. Since many centuries tourists are attracted to Indian soil because of its powerful attraction. Travel has always been one of the important means of social interaction between the nations.

Organised effort to promote tourism in India started in 1945. A committee was set up by the Government of India under Sir John Sargent, Educational Advisor, as its chairman. It submitted an interim report in 1946. The committee recommended whole time attention of a separate tourist organization which should take initiative.[10]

Environmental Aspect

In the underdeveloped and developing regions, tourism development is a powerful answer to some of the environmental problems, such as poor water supply, inadequate sanitation and sewage facilities, deficient nutrition, bad housing conditions, disease and sickness and vulnerability to national disaster. The environmental problems can be overcome, to a great extent, by controlling the country's rate of development and proper planning of tourism. The resort development should conserve a section of the land to maintain natural environment. Besides self-regulation in planning, a part of the investment should be devoted to conservation and environment to protect the natural resources from extinction and increase or expand the resources that are bestowed by nature. Tourism comprises complete system of nature which includes the man and his activities, wildlife, mountains and valleys, rivers, forests, social and cultural system, flora and fauna, weather and climate etc. The whole system requires an environmental and ecological preservation which can be achieved to a fair degree through promotion and development of tourism.

Basically, the human environment relates to people and embraces factors such as physical, psychological and ecological. The physical environment could be changed with the objective of creating a destination that is pleasant to visitors. It must totally blend into and enhance the local and natural environment. This could be achieved by using various techniques such as use of organic materials, low rise architecture and landscaping that complements the natural advantages of scenic sites and exceptional land features. Indigenous building material could be used to the maximum possible extent. Yet another means of enhancing or preserving the human environment is the historical and cultural protection. Tourism offers unlimited opportunities for bringing men and his heritage together. It builds the bridge between our past and present.

Cultural Aspect

Tourism development revives and rejuvenates the local culture too. Practically all our local artists, craftsmen, and those employed in performing arts are employed professionally, which in turn sparks off a renewal of interest of local residents in their own cultural heritage. In order to make tourism an effective means for the development of social and cultural contacts in our country, efforts need to be made in the field of education and information in tourist spending as well as tourist receiving regions.[11]

Invisible Exports

Tourism is the second largest net foreign exchange earner by way of invisible exports. Tourism creates more jobs than any other sector for every rupee invested. The endeavour of Government of India is to achieve sustained growth of tourist facilities in the private sector and to ensure high standards of quality in their services. Tourism is presently India's third largest export industry after ready made garments, gems and jewellery. The most significant feature of the tourism industry is its capacity to generate large scale employment opportunities particularly in remote and backward areas. It offers enormous potential for economically utilizing the natural attractions like landscapes, mountains, beaches, rivers etc. which would otherwise remain either idle or under utilized. It applies to a multitude of man-made attractions like monuments palaces, forts and unique rural and city environments.

Ancillary Industries

There are several ancillary industries also which are affected by the construction of hotels, textiles, furnishings, furniture, machinery, food stuffs, breweries, crockery, handicrafts etc. are some of the industries directly benefited. The industry also requires the services of professionals like architects, accountants, contractors, interior decorators etc. In a developing country like India, it is desirable that the multiple economic benefits of tourism be spread as widely as possible to nook and corner of the country.[13]

Private Investment

To attract private investment in tourism sector foreign investment is increasingly getting attracted to this sector. Major initiatives have been taken in this direction through discussion with the hotel and travelling agencies, as well as, industries in general both at the national and international level. The state governments are also trying their best to attract private investment in this sector and some states like Tamil Nadu and Andhra Pradesh have made headway in this direction.[13]

Planned Tourism Development

Considering the significance of tourism in the development of the country, the Government of India included this activity in the five year development plans. Each plan made financial allocations for the improvement of infrastructure for tourism in India. As a result, the tourism sector got a boost and India stands out as one of the major tourist attractions/destinations in the world. A brief review of the planned development of tourism is presented below:

First Five Year Plan (1951-56)

In fact there was no specific financial allocation for the development of tourism. Tourism in First Five Year Plan. The Division, formed in 1949, functioned under the Ministry of Transport and its outlay included some provision for tourism activities. These mainly related to the opening of tourist offices within the country and overseas, and the production of tourism publicity material. The Government of India tourist offices were set up at New York and London in 1952 and 1953 respectively for promoting tourist traffic to the country. The first Hotel Management Institute was set up at Bombay in 1954 for ensuring availability of manpower for tourism.[14]

Second Five Year Plan (1956-61)

There is no specific and separate allocation for tourism in the Second Plan. An outlay of Rs. 336.38 lacs was included under the transport sector in the plan for the development of tourist infrastructure both within the Central and State sectors. Second plan stipulated two types of schemes for tourism, namely, schemes for development of facilities at a limited number of places visited by foreign tourists, and schemes to provide facilities for home tourists of low and middle income groups at a limited number of places. It was also stated that the first category of schemes would be undertaken by the Centre and those in the second category would be implemented by the States with a certain measure of assistance from the Centre.[15]

Remarkably, for the first time, the government entered the hotel business by constructing Hotel Ashok at New Delhi in 1956. In order to boost tourism, the government converted the Tourism Division (Tourism Cell) operating in the Ministry of Transport into a full fledged Directorate of Tourism in 1958.

Third Five Year Plan (1961-66)

The Third Five Year Plan concentrated largely on the provision of accommodation and transport facilities. As the private sector investment in tourism sector was insufficient, the state assumed the role of an entrepreneur and invested in tourism related activities. The government established India Tourism Development Corporation (ITDC) in 1966 for development of tourism infrastructure and for promotion of tourism in the country. The plan document also makes an important distinction between central and state schemes. While schemes in the Central sector provide for facilities which are important from the point of view of foreign tourism, those in the state plans are intended mainly for home tourism.[16]

Fourth Five Year Plan (1969-74)

The Fourth Five year Plan for the first time highlighted tourism as an important means for earning foreign exchange, providing employment and promoting international contacts and understanding. Emphasis on the provision of accommodation, recreational facilities and transport was maintained. The concentration of efforts in areas identified with the larger flow of foreign tourist traffic was also maintained.[17]

Fifth Five Year Plan (1974-78)

The Fifth Five Year Plan has very cursory reference to tourism and just recommend a higher allocation for the programme. The government took measures for integrated development of some popular tourist resorts like Goa, Kovalam, Gulmarg, etc. The Fifth Five Year Plan expanded the role of the Central and State Governments. The Centre would undertake projects, which related to the promotion of international tourism and the States were advised to confine their projects to serve the needs of domestic tourists or budget tourist from overseas.[18]

Sixth Five Year Plan (1980-85)

It is pertinent to note that from the Sixth Plan new thinking on tourism in India commenced. The emphasis shifted from schemes to strategies and from foreign exchange earnings to wider issues of economic development. The plan document referred to social and economic benefits like promotion of national integration and international understanding, creation of employment, removal of regional imbalances, opening up of new growth centres in the interiors of the country, source of tax revenues for both Central and State Governments, support to local handicrafts and cultural activities, augmentation of foreign exchange earnings.[19]

The government established an apex institution namely Indian Institute of Tourism and Travel Management (IITTM), for improving availability of trained manpower in tourism sector. This period also witnessed substantial expansion of ITDC operations. The government announced the tourism promotion policy for the first time in 1982. The policy stipulated the responsibility for tourism development as a common venture of all organizations concerned with tourism in the country. The policy prescribed that Centre will be primarily responsible for promotion of international and the state sector will be concerned with domestic tourism and that the centre would play a coordinating and supplementing role towards state efforts wherever necessary. Further, tourism development cannot solely be responsibility of the government, it has to be a common endeavour of all agencies concerned with its development at central and state levels, of public sector undertaking and the private sector, of airlines, railways and communication system, municipal and local bodies, educational and cultural organizations etc. The combined effort would be directed towards achieving a comprehensive, well rounded and integrated development enabling tourism to make positive and effective contribution to the economic growth of the country.[20]

Seventh Five Year Plan (1985-90)

In the Seventh Five Year Plan tourism was given the status of an industry which implied that such business activities would in future be entitled to the some incentives and concessions as applicable to an export industry. It is for the first time in the seventh plan that tourism gets considerable attention in the plan document with a stated intention of faster development of tourism, according it the status of 'industry' and exploring its potential for sale of handicrafts and national integration.[21]

Eighth Five Year Plan (1992-97)

The major thrust in the Eighth Plan was on developing tourism mainly through private initiative. The public sector, which was the prime mover of development in the past, was to play the role of a catalyst while the private sector was expected to invest in the creation/expansion of tourism infrstructural facilities like hotels, restaurants, tourist transport etc. The Plan restricted the role of government to that of regulation, coordination and facilitation. Following the liberalization policies, the tourism industry was declared as a priority sector for foreign investment. The government has allowed automatic approvals for foreign investment with equity upto 51 per cent in tourism related project. Proposals for higher levels of equity investment are also permitted in specific cases. Investment upto 100 per cent of equity was allowed to non-resident Indians. Thus, the foreign investors could repatriate the profits and dividends and were free to engage foreign technicians and professionals. The Government of India also set up an investment cell for encouraging investment in the field of tourism. As a result, inquiries are being received relating to availability of land and other infrastructural facilities at different tourist centres, available incentives, procedural aspects involved, agencies to be contacted and clearances required etc. Various regulations to protect monuments, flora and fauna and beaches etc. are enacted and enforced by the government agencies. As the private sector is guided by the profit motive, the government will have to engage in market promotion activities to derive full national benefits out of tourism development.[22]

Ninth Five Year Plan (1997-2002)

This plan is to establish effective coordination with all relevant agencies so as to achieve synergised development. The specific components have been identified as infrastructure development, product improvement and diversification, growth of mega tourism resorts, entrepreneurship development and promotion of self employment opportunities, enhanced tourist facilitation, Human Resource Planning, research and computerization, promotion and marketing, environmental protection and cultural preservation, provision of incentives and monitoring and evaluation. The plan approach would be to concentrate on a few selected centres and circuits to achieve a balanced development of infrastructure in an integrated manner. As a result, the Central assistance for infrastructural growth wouyld be confined to identified centres and circuits each year till they are saturated. The Planning Commission has approved an outlay of Rs. 511.32 crore as budgetary support during the five year period ending 31 March, 2002.[23]

Tenth Five Year Plan (2002-2007)

It will appear from the table given below in tenth five year plan Government of India has increased the allocation to 2900 crore for tourism giving it a five-fold growth over the ninth five year plan, which is unprecedented. This also shows the significance of tourism as a contribution to economic development of India that this activity is receiving the focus of attention and consistently larger financial allocation plan after plan.[15]

TABLE 2.4

Plan Outlay from First Five Year Plan to Tenth Five Year Plan

Five Year Plans	*Tourism (Rs. in crores)*	*% of total Plan Outlay*
First Plan (1951-56)	Not mentioned	—
Second Plan (1956-61)	Not mentioned	—
Third Plan (1961-66)	4.001	0.11
Fourth Plan (1969-74)	25.00	0.30
Fifth Plan (1974-78)	23.62	0.121
Sixth Plan (1980-85)	72.00	0.15
Seventh Plan (1985-90)	138.68	0.15
Eighth Plan (1992-97)	272.00	0.11
Ninth Plan (1997-2002)	511.32	—
Tenth Plan (2002-2007)	2900.00	—

Source: Various Five Year Plans, Planning Commission, Govt. of India, New Delhi, p. 202.

Forms and Products of Indian Tourism

India is one of the oldest most complex and most fascinating civilizations in the world and a history reaching back 4000 years. It is a country of all seasons and all reasons. It is an interesting and charming India as a tourist country. For the visitor India and her history are both an inspiration and a challenge. The sheer wealth of Indian culture, its vast range and often dazzling colour has fascinated generation after generation of visitors.

India is another world and another culture. To the north of India are world's highest mountains, the mighty Himalayas ever snow capped offering heavens of unmatched beauty. On the western and eastern coastline are virgin beaches with a tropical ambience of coconut, palms and shining sands. There are backwaters, forests, animal life, fauna and flora, bird life and many more.

Thus, beautifully rich natural endowments, ancient civilization dating back to B.C., a pluralistic society consisting of different religions, cultural impact of different rulers, and above all the unmatched hospitality of its people make India a fascinating tourist destination to global visitor. It offers to the tourist various forms of tourism attraction each with multiple contents. The different forms of which India's tourism sector today consists of are mentioned below:

1. Religious Tourism
2. Cultural Tourism
3. Adventure Tourism
4. Historical Tourisms
5. Eco-Tourism.

A brief description of the contents of these forms of tourism in India is presented in the following paragraphs,

Religious Tourism

As an important tourism segment, religious tourism offers a lot of visiting attractions to tourists which include revered shrines, holy rivers, famous places of worship and pilgrimage, gods and goddesses, Durgahs, churches, etc. The Vedic literature and scripts of other religions are the fountainhead of highlighting the basic religious relics and shrines as well as their locales. People come to have 'darshan' and pay obesence to the gods and goddesses, to take a dip in the holy rivers for purity of soul, and visit shrines located on mountains and various cities of the country. India is, thus, endowed and dotted with religious places of all important religions of the world.

Hinduism is the major religion of India. This early Vedic religion had been designated by the name of Hemotheism or Monotheism, which is the belief in single Godhead. It is *Eka-Ishwarvad*. Later, it has been described as the worship of Prakriti or Primordial Energy. The chief deities of the *Rigveda* have their origin to the glorification of natural phenomenon. The worship of abstract deities like Dhatri (the establisher), Vidhatri (the ordainer), Vishwakarma (the all creating), Prajapati (the lord of creatures) etc. has remained in practice. Some scholars of Hinduism find in the hymns the names related to Shiva,

Shakti, Vak, Aditi, Prithvi, Saraswati, Shree, bhumi, etc. This suggests that both the male and female principles of Divine Godhead were adored through symbols and icons. That is why in India we find Matri Devi, Natraj, Ganesha, Surya, Vishnu, Laxmi, Nandi, Shesha Naga and other deities in the places of worship for tourists. More prominently is the worship of Devi Durga alongwith Shiva found in the religious thoughts of Hindus, popularly known as Sanatan Dharma.

Some of the major temples and important religious centres make India as religious tourism destinations. The world's greatest Sufi shrine Khwaja Moinuddin Chishti, lies in Ajmer. Another pilgrimage centre for Muslims are Durgahs of Hazrat Nizamuddin Aulia at Delhi, Hazrat Sabir Sahib at Kalyar, etc.

Jainism founded by Lord Rishabh is one of the oldest living religions of the world. The fundamental principles of Jainism are Ahimsa, Aparigraha, Anekant, and the Law of Karma. The Jains have built some of the most exquisite temples in Ranakpur, Mount Abu, Shri Mahavirjee, Osiam Jaisalmer, Chittorgarh and other parts of India.

There is also a large majority of Christians, Muslims and Sikhs to give India a cosmopolitan flavour. The followers of these religions and their rulers over the period, were instrumental in constructing a number of very important mosques, churches and temples which are built in their religious style in different parts of the country. Some of the most exquisite carvings on marble stone and wood were created by the believers and exist to this day as a living proof of the creative genius which continue as great fascinations by its sheer brilliance. Other than the religious satisfaction, the structure themselves and the very surroundings of these holy places actually give the tourist/visitor a sense of serene peace and calm.

The religious tourism is most common amongst domestic visitors who go place to place in the country to perform this ritual periodically. Foreigners of the identical religion and sects also visit these shrines, have a look of their revered gods and goddesses, visit various temples and Durgahs periodically. All this makes religious tourism as an important and big segment of India's tourism industry.

Cultural Tourism

Tourism is a multidimensional industry with heterogenous segments for the visitors and cultural tourism offers irresistible temptation to the tourist to visit India. Cultural tourism presents to the visitor attractions which include most importantly archaeological structures representing the varied civilizations of India. Arts and crafts, Painting, folks Music and Dances, Fairs and Festivals, Indian cinemas, national Parks and Sanctuaries, etc. The contents of cultural tourism are briefly described below.

Art and Craft

As far as the field of Art and Craft is concerned, India is among the richest country in the world. Indian peple over the year have sharpened the creative senses, artistic skills and have created a richest treasure of art and craft. Stone clay, leather, wood, glass, brass, silver, gold and textiles were given the most brilliant forms by the Indian artists. For women, there is infinite variety like tie and dye fabrics, embroidered garments, enamel jewellery inlayed with precious and semi-precious stones and leather items. Rajasthan has its own special crafts. Some of their popular crafts are meenakari, jewellery, ivory, glass work, sandalwood and wood work, stone work, blue pottery, hand block printing, tie and dye terracotta sculptures, paintings or camel hydes, embroidery, cloth paintings, carpets, durries, inlay workers on brass and wood to be found all over India are the basic attraction to international tourists.

Paintings

The decoration of dwellings and other household objects are some aspects of creative genius of India. The miniature painting is perhaps the most fascinating and distinctive styles that have existed here and are renowned the world over.

Different schools of painting have flourished in India since sixteenth century and each has name and fame in the distinct style of painting. For instance, Kotah-Bundi school transferred to the paintings the flooring rivers, dense forests, and lush green fields of that region. The Kishangarh school is best known for its Bani Thani paintings depicting long necks, large almond shape eyes, long fingers and the use of subdued colours. Jodhpur has a very strong folk tradition and here the figures are mainly robust warriors and dainty woman. Paintings of the legendary lovers like Dhola-Maru on camel back, hunting scenes which included innumerable horses and elephants dominate the paintings of Marwar region. Similarly Bikaner too had strong Mughal influences and developed their own style. Paintings on wall of palaces and inner chambers of forts are well known all over the world. Cloth paintings of India which include the phads scroll paintings used by the Bhopas and the Pichwais are also very popular among the tourists.

Folk Music and Dance

There is gay abundance in India in the form of dancing, singing, Drama, Devotional music and puppet shows and other community festivities which transforms the hardworking Indian into a few loving and carefree individual. Each region has its own folk, entertainment and the dance styles. Interestingly enough, even the musical instruments in different parts of the country are different. Professional performers like the Bhaats, Dholis, Merasis, Nats, Bhopas and Bhands and many others are present across the country. Some of the better known forms of entertainment are ghoomer Dance, Gair Ghoomer, Gair, Ghari Dance, Kachni Ghodi, Fir Dance, Drum Dance, Teerah Taali, Kathputli, Pabuji Ki Panad, Maand etc.

Fairs and Festivals

Every religion in India has its own festivals. In addition to the festivals celebrated by Hindus, Muslims and others, there are also the traditional fairs in which all people participate and they are really an enjoyment. There are religious fairs, there are animal fairs and there are fairs to mark the changing season. Other than these traditional fairs, there are established festivals which involve elephants, camel race, boat race, processions to mark religion events, dance and music, which are special attraction for the tourists from time to time. In fact, fairs and festivals celebrations occur almost round the year and are an splendid opportunity for the visitor to gain an insight into the life.

Indian Cuisine

Each region in India has its own traditional dishes and specialities. Indian cuisines have evolved over the course of its history. The recipes have been handed down through the generations by demonstrations and word of mouth. Mughals in sixteenth century were fond of good living, cooking and eating. Muslim cooking is based on meat. Their influence is strongest in north and central India where Mughal dishes evolved into an important cullinary art and is part of Indian cuisine. Extreme south cooking is mainly vegetarian. The cooking habits of India vary according to religious communities and area to area.

The heart of Indian cooking is Masala (spices). It is a mixture of spices called 'garam masala'. Game birds are a delicacy, teetur and batair are special favourite dish. Some of the popular fishes eaten are pomfret, rohu, Bombay duck, Indian salmon, trout, shrimps, prawns, crab, etc. Indian breads are prepared with different cooking methods such as poories, kachories, nans, sheermal, Bakar khani, Paratha, bhaturas, etc. The popular methods of cooking are boiling and frying. Traditional method used is split roasting.

Every Indian meal is a feast in itself and makes the tourist voracious for Indian varieties of food. The food is rich in proteins and vitamins besides being tastiest and davity.

National Parks and Sanctuaries

India stores huge wildlife because of its topography. There are barren deserts, scrub thorn arid forests, rocks and ravines as well as wet lands and lush green forests. And each of these areas houses a large variety of animal and bird life, some of them are rare while some endangered. Some parts of India are the home for tigers, black bucks, chinkara, the rare desert fox, the endangered caracal, the great Indian bustard gavial, monitor lizard, wild boars, porcupines. Migrating birds like the common crane, ducks, coots, pelicans and the rare Siberian cranes, imperial sand grouses, falcons, buzzards, flock to India during winter months.

India proudly can boast of eleven National Parks, over two dozen sanctuaries and two closed areas. Most of these areas are open to visitors round the year but are closed briefly during the monsoons. These National parks and Sactuaries are spread in various parts of the country and looked after by the Wildlife Department of the Government. Gir National Park for animals especially the Asiatic Tiger, Ghana Bird Sactuary Bharatpur, Corbett National Park are of special interest to tourists.

Adventure Tourism

The idea of conquering the nature and revealing the mysteries of it has always been a desire of the human mind. Based on this human instinct is the adventure tourism. India offers interesting opportunities of adventures to tourists. The country is richly endowed with mountains, deserts, sea beaches, rivers, marshy sands, jungles, forests, which make it a chosen country of the nature. The geography of the country is sufficiently endowed so as to attract tourists with an adventurous zeal.

Adventure tourism consists of many activities such as rock climbing, trekking, river rafting, mountaineering, skiing, paragliding, etc. Modern adventure tourism additionally include water sports, canoing and kayaking.

Trekking: It is a very low cost adventure activity. It is the best way to explore the mountain ranges on foot. Himalayan ranges present a unique option for trekkers. There are many unique spots to explore in the Himalayas.

Valley of Flowers in Uttarakhand region is trekkers' paradise. The scenic attraction of this place is marvelous with flowers surrounded on all sides with sloppy mountains. The trek to this place is quite tiresome. Trekkers enjoys this spot as the path is fraught with dense forests, tributaries of river Ganga gushing in full flow with exotic herbs and shrubs on the way besides steep mountains.

There are also places of pilgrimage situated on the hill tops. Hemkunt Sahib is one such place for Sikhs situated six kms above the Valley of Flowers. The path is very steep, at times glacier blocking the way and adding to scenic beauty of the area. On the whole trekkers have to tread about 2 kms of the mountainous path to reach this spot.

Yamunotri is another one of the four pious spots in Uttarakhand. This spot can be reached by trekking 13 kms of mountainous terrain. The beauty of Yamunotri is excellent.

Many other trekking routes full of scenic beauty and places of pilgrimage are there for the tourists to enjoy in various parts of the country.

Skiing: It is another major sport in adventure tourism. Gulmarg in Kashmir has been an internationally acclaimed spot for this sport. Auli in Joshimut is another such spot. It has the state of the art technology for this sport. It provides the facilities of skilift, comfortable cabin and restaurants.

Dyara Bugyal, situated at 3190 mts. above sea level in Uttaranchal, too, offers a unique opportunity for skieng. During winter a thick layer of snow covers the area around 2 sq.kms which is ideal for lovers of this sport. The spot provides a picturesque view which is second to none.

Dal Lake of Kashmir in a frozen state provides a fun sport for children and amateurs alike.

Mountaineering: A very fascinating sport for the tourists interested in adventure tourism. The steep mountains of Uttarkashi and Rohtang Pass, Chandrakhani in Himachal Pradesh are excellent spots for mountaineering.

Nehru Institute of Mountaineering is a pioneer institute which attracts a number of persons both from within and abroad.

River Rafting: There exists a tremendous potential for this sport in India. The river Ganges from Rishikesh to Rudraprayag provides an excellent flow for this sport. Rivers such as Teerta in North Bengal, Brahamputra in Assam, Beas in Manali and

Indus in Ladakh provide an excellent condition for the river rafters.

Water sports: India has a very long coastline. The Coromandal Coast and Malabar coast are well known all over the world. These two areas are ideal places for Kakaying, cannoning and many other water sports. Indian coastal areas are also blessed with luxuriant natural beauty.

There are also a number of lakes where water sports for the tourists could be available. Orissa and Kerala are famous for their lakes. Kashmir's Dal Lake is not behind anyone in water sports. These aquatic regions are ideal for adventure tourism including international aquatic events.

Heritage Tourism

India is a country on which rulers of various faiths and religions have ruled. Its history is divided into ancient period, medieval period, and the modern period. These periods are marked by the rule of different dynasties who governed this country for years and centuries. Each dynasty has left imprints of the culture and civilization of the period in the form of palaces and monuments. At a time there were different rulers ruling over different parts of the country. If in the north, the Mughals ruled, the Marathas ruled in the west, south was ruled by others and over the eastern region a different dynasty ruled.

India possesses a rich heritage of these rulers in the form of huge imposing stately buildings reminiscent of the glorious heritage of their period. Every region of India possesses such historical attractions that are irresistible to the tourists both domestically and internationally. Taj Mahal in Agra is among the seventh wonders of the world. Built by the Mughal Emperor Shahjahan in memory of is beloved queen Mumtaz Mahal, the musoleum is a structure of white marble carved in flowers and petals inlayed with precious stones and jewels. The Taj is a unique marble structure whose beauty lies in the moonlight when it shines milky and so beautiful that it is irresistible for a visitor not to see it time and again. Many visitors, particularly, women tourists envy that if such a grand marble tomb could be built for them, they are prepared to die for its sake.

Fatehpur Sikri in Sikandra, Agra Fort, Jama Masjid at Delhi, Red Fort at Delhi, Qutub Minar at Delhi, Ashok Pillar at Delhi and many other historical buildings at Lucknow and other places in northern India make a special historical attraction for the tourists.

In the west and south India, very rich historical vestiges exist. The palaces of Nizam of Hyderabad, the forts of the Tipu in Karnataka, the tombs of Sultans in Andhra Pradesh, Gol Gumbad at Bijapore, the Ajanta and Ellora caves in Maharashtra, and grand places of Rajputana (Rajasthan) and many other historical monuments are worthy to mention. The Konark Temples in Orissa and Buddhist Monasteries in Sikkim and Ladakh are other historical spots which draw tourists from the world over.

Thus, historically India is second to none in tourism. It adds to the pleasure of the tourist that he moves from place to place and enjoy the hospitality and ambience of every region while having a full glimpse of India when he visits the historical endowments of the country.

Ecotourism

Ecotourism is the latest emergent theme. It expresses the need for ecological harmony. Ecotourism has emerged simply because all forms of development and activity including tourism have damaging impact on the environment. Tourism to be sustainable require initiative about protection of environment. Tourism depends upon the existence of environments in locations which are perceived as being scenic, attractive and desirable. This creates a relationship between tourism and environment. Therefore, all the stakeholder in tourism development should safeguard the natural environment with a view to achieving sound, continuous and sustainable economic growth.

India's tourist attractions ranging from forts, caves, hill stations, beaches, pilgrimage centres, forest reserves and wildlife sanctuaries must be developed while keeping the ecological considerations in mind. The conservation and development of world heritage sites, Ajanta and Ellora, certain sites in Kerala, Goa, Rajasthan, Uttarakhand, Himachal Pradesh, Madhya Pradesh and West Bengal has started following the basic principles and practices of Ecotourism. The Central government with the help of state governments and NGOs has initiated special ecotourism ventures to develop and promote the eco-potential base for the states to the domestic and international tourist clientele.

Tourism, basically, being a service industry developing nations must take necessary steps to build a pool of efficiently trained people to fill various jobs which will be created subsequently. To manage various tourist services a variety of jobs will have to be created. For successful tourism development, efficient and professional management, quality of staff training is essential. Quality of staff training is often relatively neglected during early stages of tourism sector development. In the case of India which is a developing country, it will be appropriate to study volume of manpower required for activities complementary to accommodation industry, in particular in commercial sector. In case there is expansion of facilities and services, special care has to be taken to ensure that there will be no shortage of trained and well qualified personnel. A staff planning may be done to determine need for various personnel required. This involves a series of activities such as job analysis, job descriptions, job specifications and staff forecasts. This lead to a detailed forecast of exactly what types of personnel, with which qualifications and skills will be required. Programmes should be prepared to screen and train existing personnel so that they could acquire technical and attitudinal skills. Technical skills include food and beverage production and service, system analysis and design, facility and equipment operation and maintenance, administration, personnel management and financial management. Attitudinal skills include adaptability, pride judgement and flexibility. This helps in determining whether there is a need for trained personnel from foreign or local people are to be sent for training to other countries or not.[25]

Tourism is the single largest foreign exchange earner to

more than 30 countries and India is keen to reap its potential of tourism to this end. Tourism sector has capacity to generate large-scale employment opportunities in the accommodation sector, transport sector, food service areas and many more such areas, which are essential towards making the stay of the tourists comfortable. In the year 2000, tourism industry generated 192 million jobs, benefiting developed and emerging economies. The right person in the right job is essential for the success in any business. Tourism industry also requires trained and skilled manpower for quality and efficiency of service which is done through proper and effective Human Resource Planning.[26]

India has great tourism potentials for it is our unique diversification of cultural and natural attractions which contribute the resources for this industry. India has an ancient civilization that is preserved in its religion, customs, traditions and architecture. Its traditional dances and music are loved by all. A unique asset of tourism is that there is no shortage of raw materials. India's unique variety of cultural and natural attractions constitute the resources for this industry.

Tourism needs variety and India with its vast dimensions and diversity offers to every class of visitor something not found elsewhere from the snake charmer to the eternal snowcapped peaks of the Himalayas and system of the folk dances to the big game hills. Due to this reason it can be concluded that India have very flourishing future in tourism.

But highly skilled and trained manpower is the need of hour for all-dimensional expansion and development of Tourism in India.

REFERENCES

1. Makhija, B.N. (1996), 'Tourism Planning in India', *Yojana*, New Delhi, August, pp. 29-31.
2. Bezbaruah, M.P. (1999), 'Tourism – Current Scenario and Future Prospects', *Yojana*, New Delhi, August, pp. 7-14.
3. 'Tourism: Potential for Growth and Employment', *Yojana*, New Delhi, December, 1995, p. 13.

4. Bezbaruah, M.P. (1999), 'Tourism – Current Scenario and Future Prospects', *Yojana*, New Delhi, August, pp. 7-14.
5. Seth, Rabindra, (1996), 'Tourism in India: An Overview', *Yojana*, New Delhi, August, pp. 19-21.
6. Dharmarajan, S. (1999), 'Tourism: An Instrument for Development', *Yojana*, New Delhi, August, pp. 15,17,19,46.
7. Rehman, S.S.H. (1996), 'Strategy for Boosting Tourism', *Yojana*, New Delhi, August, pp. 17-18.
8. 'Tourism: Potential for Growth and Employment', *Yojana*, New Delhi, December, 1995, pp. 13, 20.
9. Seth, Rabindra, (1998), 'Tourism: Opportunities for Growth, *Yojana*, New Delhi, August, pp. 75-77.
10. Rao, R.A. Padmanabha, (1999), 'Tourism: Medium of Social and Cultural Development', *Yojana*, New Delhi, August, pp. 3-39, 41.
11. Negi, Jagmohan, (1996), 'Tourism and Development: Some Issues', *Yojana*, New Delhi, August, pp. 33-37.
12. Rao, RA. Padmanabha (1999), 'Tourism: Medium of Social and Cultural Development', *Yojana*, New Delhi, August, pp. 35-39, 41.
13. Seth, Mira (1996), 'Tourism in India: Some Thrust Areas', *Yojana*, New Delhi, August, pp. 7-9.
14. Makhija, B.N. (1996), 'Tourism Planning in India', *Yojana*, New Delhi, August, pp. 29-31.
15. Ranga, Mukesh (2003), *Tourism Potential in India*, Abhijeet Publications, Delhi, p. 72.
16. Makhija, B.N., (1996), 'Tourism Planning in India', *Yojana*, New Delhi, August, pp. 29-31.
17. Singh, Percy, K. (1998), 'Fifty Years of Indian Tourism', Kanishka, New Delhi, pp. 71-72.
18. Ranga Mukesh, *op.cit.*, p. 74.
19. Bezbaruah, M.P., (1999), 'Tourism – Current Scenario and Future Prospects', *Yojana*, New Delhi, August, pp. 7-14.
20. Makhija, B.N. (1996), 'Tourism Planning in India'. *Yojana*, New Delhi, August, pp. 29-31.
21. Ranga, Mukesh, *op.cit.*, pp. 75-77.
22. Makhija, B.N. (1996), 'Tourism Planning in India', *Yojana*, New Delhi, August, pp. 29-31.
23. Dharmarajan, S. (1999), 'Tourism: An Instruments for Development', *Yojana*, New Delhi, August, pp. 15,17, 19,46.
24. Raina, Chaman Lal and Abhinav K. Raina (2005), *Fundamental of*

Tourism and Indian Religion – Principles and Practices, Kanishka, New Delhi, p. 47.

25 . Sarkar, Arun Kumar and Dhar, Premnath (1998), *Indian Tourism – Economic Planning and Strategies*, Kanishka, New Delhi, pp. 270-271.

26 . Ranga, Mukesh and Devesh Nigam (2003). *New Approaches in Tourism Management*, Abhijeet Publications, Delhi, pp. 80-81.

3

Human Resource Planning: Theoretical Perspective

The previous chapter presented a profile of the Indian Tourism sector which showed that the sector is highly rich in offering huge opportunities for the tourists to visit India. The country is endowed with varied tourist attractions like historical, cultural, adventure, religious, and other sorts of tourism. As a result the number of tourists arrival has been consistently on increase and the rate of growth continues to soare. The tourism sector is also an important invisible contributor of foreign exchange to the country. However, much more can be achieved and the tourism sector may get a boost if the development of manpower is made in a scientific and systematic manner. This chapter accordingly is devoted to Human Resource Planning aspect of tourism industry in India. It analyses and discusses the different aspects of Human Resource Planning in the tourism sector.

What is Human Resource Planning?

During the first part of 20th century, the focus in human resource planning was on the hourly production worker for increasing efficiency with the need to improve productivity and to introduce greater objectivity to personnel policies. In the 60's prevailing view of Human Resource Planning was that tourism industry forecasted their needs, identified the gaps between what could be needed and what was available. Manpower planners planned for recruitment, selection and placement of new employees, provided for training and development and anticipated necessary promotion end transfers. During 80s, human resource planning, the employees desire for participation in decisions that affected their work and careers become stronger. In 90s' concepts in vogue were job sharing, reduced working hours, flexibility of time, significant reshaping of work and work customs, job design, job enrichment, empowerment, total quality management and business process re-engineering.

Effective human resource planning now is identified as a process of analyzing an organisation's human resource needs under changing conditions and developing the activities necessary to satisfy these needs.

Human Resource Planning also refers to the process including forecasting, developing and controlling by which a firm ensures that it has the right number of people and the right kind of people at the right places, at the right time doing work for which they are economically most useful.[1] Thus, Human Resource Planning consists of projecting future manpower requirements and developing manpower plans for the implementation of the projects.

Tourism sector employees and volunteers need to be recognized as its valued ambassadors. They are, possibly, the most single factor in ensuring the successful management of tourism. It is, therefore, essential that the vital nature of the service that employees provide to visitors be recognized. Front-line workers especially, such as rangers and staff in visitor centers, are the visible public expression of the management philosophy behind the tourism sector's operation. If the relationship between staff and visitors is positive, the benefits will be many.

In a well-run organization, management knows about its staff. It should have access to data on its labour force, especially about recruitment and turnover rates, as well as being generally informed about the welfare of its workforce. Good human resource planning and development create a workforce that is more likely to succeed. Therefore, tourism sector authorities that are committed to researching, hiring and developing their personnel by using appropriate Human Resource Planning strategies will be better placed to protect the environment, involve local communities and share the conservation message with tourists. If the staff are selected carefully and skillfully trained, tourism industry will operate more smoothly and tourists will undoubtedly notice, appreciate and share their appreciation with other potential visitors.

There are general trends in the labour force at large that can be used to improve human resource planning, recruiting and paying. In most countries, statistics on employment participation rates are compiled by national statistics agencies. This index is a measure of the proportion of people eligible for inclusion in the labour force who are actually in it, and can be used to protect labour force availability within different employment sectors. By comparing the participation rate with population demographics, a planner is able to identify which segments of the labour force to target to increase the success of recruitment efforts.

In many countries including India, there are wide variations between the availability of technically trained manpower and the actual demand for such personnel. On one hand, there may be severe shortage of technicians and engineers necessary for development and on the other hand there may be a surplus of certain types and levels of personnel. The problem is not confined to developing countries alone. Despite the high level of their development efforts, the developed countries still have critical manpower shortages. These are no less serious than the problems confronting the less developed countries, but they are the consequences of a different set of imperatives or pressures. HRP differs from Human Resource Planning – it focuses both on the quantitative and qualitative aspects.

Thus, at the national level, a proper and comprehensive HRP effort can help us identify the levels of skills, knowledge and attitude of the young graduates passing out in different disciplines, make a qualitative comparison of these with those of other nations, and realize those skills, knowledge and attitudes which are lacking with us or those which are our strong points.

Systematic analysis of manpower resources have to be continuously made. For this, databanks have to be set up with all relevant information regarding personnel in different grades, their educational qualification, their experience, special aptitude, etc. Forecast of manpower requirements will have to be made keeping in mind the trends in productivity and business environment.

The key to effective human resource planning is the analysis of the factors representing change – change that potentially affects survival, growth, efficiency and effectiveness, as well as excellence, productivity and profitability of business.[2]

Manpower planning and human resource planning are synonymous. In the past, the phrase manpower planning was widely used, but now the emphasis is on human resource planning which is more broad based.

According to Stainer, "Human Resource Planning is the strategy for the acquisition, utilisation, improvement and preservation of an organisation's human resources. It is aimed at coordinating the requirements for and the availability of different types of employees".[3]

Coleman has defined Human Resource Planning as "the process of determining manpower requirements and the means for meeting those requirements in order to carry out the integrated plan of the organisation."[4]

According to Gardon McBeath, Human Resource Planning involves two stages. The first stage is concerned with the detailed planning of manpower requirements for all types and levels of employees throughout the period of plan, and the second stage is concerned with planning of manpower supplies to provide the organisation with the right types of peoples from all sources to meet the planned requirements.[5]

Beach defined human resource planning as "a process of determining and assuming that the organisation will have an adequate number of qualified persons available at the proper times performing jobs which meet the needs of the enterprise and which provide satisfaction for the individuals involved."[6]

According to Wickstrom, Human Resource Planning consists of a series of activities, viz.[7]

(a) Forecasting future manpower requirements, either in terms of mathematical projections of trends in the economic environment and developments in industry, or in terms of judgemental estimates based upon the specific future plan of a company;

(b) Making an inventory of present manpower resource and assessing the extent to which these resources are employed optimally;

(c) Anticipating manpower problems by projecting present resources into the future and comparing them with the forecast of requirements to determine their adequacy, both quantitatively and qualitatively; and

(d) Planning the necessary programmes of requirements, selection, training, development, utilization, transfer, promotion, motivations and compensation to ensure that future manpower requirements are properly met.

Velter defined human resource planning or Human Resource Management as, "the process by which management determines how an organisation should move from its current manpower position to its desired manpower position. Through it management strives to have the right number and the right kind of people at the right places, at the right time, doing things which result in both the organisation, and the individual receiving, maximum long-range benefit".[8]

Thus it is clear from the above definitions that Human Resource Planning consists of projecting future manpower requirements and developing manpower plans for implementation of the projections. This planning cannot be rigid or static. It is amenable to modification, review and adjustments in accordance with the need of an organisation or the changing circumstances.

Human Resource Planning is the first step in any effective human resource programme. It involves predicting future human resource needs and planning the steps necessary to meet these needs. Effective human resources planning is a process of analysing an organisation's human resources needs under changing conditions and developing activities necessary to satisfy these needs. Essentially, it is a method for determining future manpower requirements and developing action plans for meeting them. Human Resource Planning is part of firm's total resource planning. It influences and is influenced by the firm's business plans, interacts with organisation plans, and contributes to business decisions.

The Government of India, recognised the importance of Human Resource Planning and set up the Institute of Applied Manpower Research, which aims at providing a broad perspective of requirements of trained manpower for economic development in different fields. The institute is also required to arrange for facilities for advanced training in Human Resource Planning to develop methods for training and building up the existing workforce, to evolve methods of identifying and developing talented persons and, generally, to secure the most effective utilisation of the country's human resources.

In the Third Five Year Plan, the Planing Commission observed as follows:

> "Of all the resources for development, perhaps the most fundamental at the present time is trained manpower.... The extent of manpower available and the training facilities established constitute a major determinants of the measure of advance which can be achieved in different directions... in each field personnel requirements have to be estimated carefully and over a long period. This calls for improved statistical information and development of techniques of manpower assessment so that the necessary estimates can be made with reasonable accuracy and a comprehensive picture build up for the economy as a whole.... Human Resource Planning is, thus, an integral part of the economic plans formulated by the Central and State Governments and their agencies and, within their own specific fields, by industrial associations and other organisations representing different activities or interests as well as by individual undertakings and institutions".[9]

Human Resource Planning ranges overall activities of the department including recruitment, selection, placement, training, education, wage and salary administration, labour welfare, industrial relations and the like. This view obviously is considerably broader than viewing manpower planning as programming the staffing of the organisation.

Human Resource Planning is the system which ensures availability of men in terms of quality and quantity as and when they are required over a period of time. There are organisations which have worked out their manpower requirements ranging from a period of three years to ten to fifteen years. Human Resource Planning is the first and most important step to be taken with regard to the effective utilisation of human resources. The system of Human Resource Planning would lead to better selection of people and effective job assignment. It would also manage to review performance of its employees. It would help in matters like transfers and promotions and in organising proper training activities.

Human Resource Planning represents an attempt to prepare for the future. Human Resource Planning provides the knowledge about present resources that an organisation must have in order to adopt adequately to sudden changes in such factors as technological advances, new markets, political and economic pressure etc.

Downsizing of manpower gives the correct picture about the number of people to be employed to complete given task in the predetermined period. It is used for achieving fundamental growth in the concern. It can work out the correct man on a correct price by the resource building or capacity building. It aims at correct place, correct man on a correct job.

As such, Human Resource Planning is must to make the optimum utilisation of the greatest resource available i.e. manpower for the success of any organisation.[10]

Dimensions of Human Resource Planning

At the national or community level, human resource planning has to deal with population, educational level and facilities, job opportunities, economic and industrial factors, paramount national or community objectives.

At the industrial undertaking level, human resource planning has to deal with certain very concrete, specific factors of the enterprise, such as its industrial products, skill requirements, and the time-frame of its production and marketing activities. But, all the same, the concern with broader things like the industrial infrastructure, educational level and facilities, political condition in the community, job market area wage structure is inevitable.

More specifically, the important dimensions of human resource planning are:

(a) *Numerical:* How many men from within the undertaking and how many from outside and at what levels of skill etc. are, important questions that human resource planning has to answer. The total number of personnel available, this could be obtained from the pay rolls and other personnel record, such as the applications for employment. The total number has to be classified on some basis, such as manual worker (i.e. daily rated, weekly rated, or monthly rated); clerical employees, ministerial staff, managers and other executives, specialists and skilled and unskilled workers, sexwise distribution etc.

(b) *Trades:* What are the trades (traditional or modern ones), which different trades could be combined to afford flexibility and interchangeability in operations, etc, have also to be established.

(c) *Skill:* Within each trade, what levels of skill are necessary now and later, and how much later – how much skill, and in which grades, can be generated by on the job training within the industry? These are some of the considerations which are very vital to human resource planning.

(d) *Time:* Human resource planning can be rendered meaningless if the time dimension is not fully considered, and integrated in the planning. When and at what stage of operation, are the men to be engaged; if training is required what lead time must be provided so that the required number of trained personnel are available at the right time, are factors which just cannot be ignored.

(e) *Motivation:* What use are the men – in right numbers with right skills and at right time – if they are not willing to give their best? Therefore, human resource planning in broader sense, must also include recommendations for proper wages, working conditions and just and fair treatment at the workplace so as to create and maintain an environment at the workplace which will motivate the men to give their best.[11]

(f) *Qualification and Experience:* The educational qualification and the professional skill desired, such as person having experience of 5 years or 10 years in a particular branch/job; and whether educationally qualified being under-graduate, post-graduate, or MBA, or graduates in Science, Commerce, Arts, Engineering or professional diploma holders, etc.; or with specialised skill and knowledge in the field of marketing, finance, computer programming or engineering work.

(g) *Job-family:* A detailed job description for each position such as stenographer who may belong to various departments, e.g. personnel, finance, marketing, general administration, and public relations etc.

(h) Compensation/salary range/pay-scales.

(i) Age groupings: Employees available in present departments, say in the age-groups 20-29 years, 30-45 years, 46 years and above.[12]

Human Resource Information System (HRIS)

Organisations are now maintaining Human Resource Information system in order to effectively manage and deal with their human resource aspect. Human Resource Information System (HRIS) is a systematic procedure for collecting, storing, maintaining, retrieving and validating data needed by an organisation about its human resources. Human Resource

Information System (HRIS) is a part of the organisation's larger Management Information System (MIS). Human Resource Information System need not be complex or even computerised. But computerisation has its own advantage of providing more accurate and timely data for decision-making. It helps for efficient and effective management of human resources in an organisation.

Need of Human Resource Information System (HRIS): Need arises of Human Resource Information System (HRIS) due to several factors, some of which are given below:

(i) Clear definition of goals.

(ii) Efficient and effective management of human resources in an organisation.

(iii) Availability of accurate and timely information about its human resources.

(iv) Career planning and counselling at all levels.

(v) To respond to ever changing statutory and other environment.

(vi) Capable for strategic planning.

(vii) Low cost of stored human resource data.

(viii) Implementation of training programme in an organisation.

(ix) Development of individual through performance, rewards and training.

(x) Allowances and deductions from compensation package.

(xi) Development of performance standards.

(xii) Flexibility for changes in environment.

(xiii) Capability to quick and effective problem-solving.

(xiv) Integration of records and files for fast retrieval, forecasting and cross-referencing.

(xv) To comply with statutory requirements.

(xvi) Transfers, promotions and organisational analysis, etc.

Process of Manpower /Human Resource Planning

Human resource process starts from planning. Human resource planning considers matching all jobs and individuals in future. The organisation can achieve this by taking systematic human resource planning. The process of human resource planning entails consideration of several steps with relevant inputs before human resource demand can be arrived at on the one hand, and identification of the source of supply to meet the demand taking into consideration the constraints on the other hand. Various stages involved in human resource planning are given below:

(i) *Deciding Goals or Objectives of Human Resource Planning:* Human Resource planning fulfils individual, organisational and national goals; but, according to Sikula, "the ultimate mission or purpose is to relate future human resources to future enterprise needs so as to maximise the future return on investment in human resources.[13]

Fig. 3.1: Human Resource Planning Process

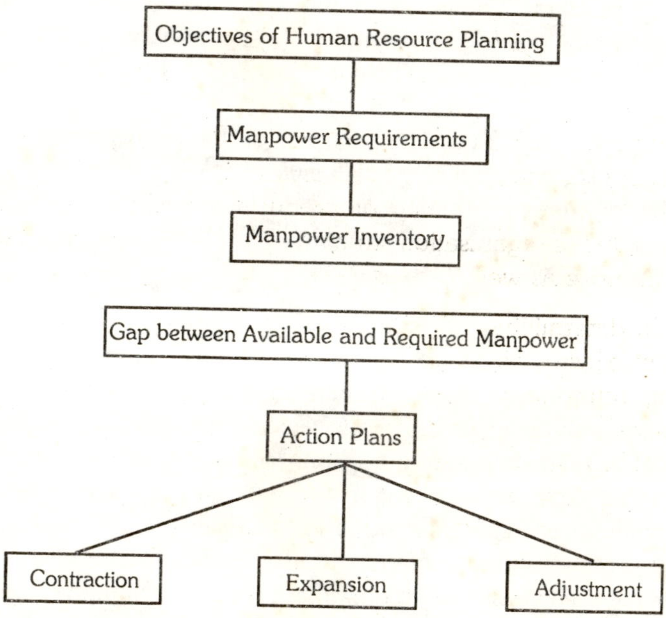

Source: Coleman, Bruce P. (1970), 'An Integrated System for Human Resource Planning', *Business Horizons,* Volume 13, p. 25.

The chief objective of Human Resource Planning is one of matching or fitting employee abilities to enterprise requirements, with an emphasis on future instead of present arrangements. Human resource plans need to be based on organisational objectives. In practice, this implies that objectives of the human resource plan must be derived from organisational objectives. Specific requirements in terms of number and characteristics of employees should be derived from the organisational objectives.

(ii) *Forecasting the Manpower Requirements:* Estimating the future quantity and quality of personnel required. Many environmental factors affect this estimation. They include business forecasts, expansion and growth, design and structural changes, management philosophy, government policy, product and human skills mix and competition. Forecasting is necessary for various reasons, such as: (a) The eventualities and contingencies of general economic business cycles (such as inflation, wages, prices, costs etc.) have an influence on the short-range and long-run plans of all organisations, (b) An expansion following enlargement and growth in business involves the use of additional personnel, and a reallocation of facilities, all of which call for advance planning of human resources, (c) changes in management philosophies and leadership skill styles,(d) Very, often, changes in the quantity or quality of products or services require a change in the organisation structure. Plans have to be made for this purpose as well.

In determining the requirements of human resources, the expected losses which are likely to occur through labour turnover–quits, retirement, death, transfers, promotions, demotions, dismissals, disability, resignations, lay-offs, and other separations–should be taken into account. Changes in human quality resulting from the experience gained in the jobs during the period and the training achieved also need to be considered. The addition of new projects also influence the demand estimates of human resources. The basic fact to remember is that the human resource in an organisation constantly changes in terms of its present and future size. Additional human resources are gained through new employment of personnel, promotions, transfers and demotions; but personnel is lost through voluntary quits, death, dismissals, terminations and retirements.

After making adjustments for wastage, anticipated and expected losses and separations, the real shortage or surplus may be found out. If a shortage is there, efforts are made to meet it either by new recruitment or promotion from within, or by developing the existing staff. If there is a surplus, it is to be decided how it will be dealt with, i.e., whether there should be transfers, lay-offs, retrenchment or reduction in the hours of work of all.[14]

(iii) *Human Resource Inventory or Forecasting Supply of Human Resources.*

It is estimates of the number and kinds of personnel that can be expected to constitute an organisation's workforce at some future point in time. It is based on a careful assessment of an organisations current supply, plus consideration of employee movement into an out of organisations.

Supply analysis covers existing human resources, internal sources of supply and external sources of supply.

Internal sources includes transfers, promotions and demotions.

Manpower inventory helps in determining and evaluating the quantity and quality of the internal human resources. It reveals what exists in stock of manpower and what can be expected in future. It also indicates the possible shortfalls in comparison with expansion requirements and the future organisation structure.

Once the present human resources are assessed the changes likely to occur therein can be estimated. Potential losses of human resources can arise in the form of resignations, discharge, or dismissals, deaths, retrenchments or lay-off, terminations, demotions, promotions, transfers, injury, ill health, deputations out, consultancy out, absenteeism.

Similarly, additions to human resources may occur in the form of new recruits, promotions, demotions, transfers deputations in, consultancy in, acquisition of new skills through training, etc.

Fig. 3.2: Human Resource Flows in a Tourism Organisation

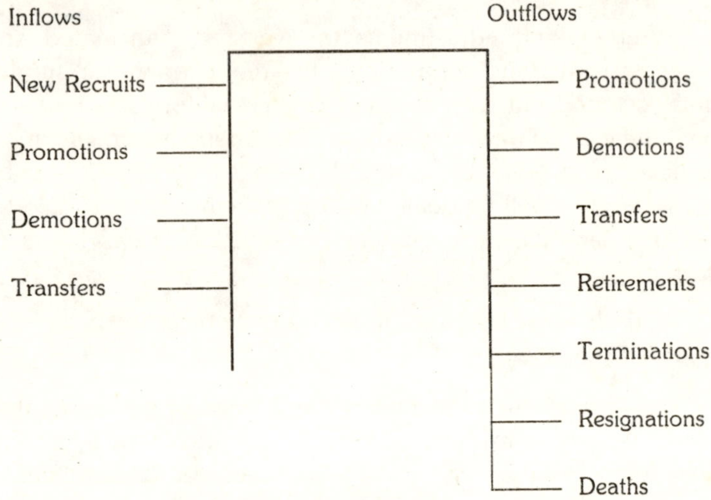

Source: Gupta, C.B. (2000), *Human Resource Management*, p. 211.

(iv) *Identification of Gap between Available and Required Human Resources:* Once an organisation's human resources requirements and supply are forecast, the two must be compared.

Such comparison will reveal either deficit or surplus of human resources in future. Such comparison helps in order that vacancies can be filled by the right employees at the right time.

(v) *Action Plans*

After identification of the human resources gaps plans are prepared to bridge these gaps. Plans to meet the surplus human resources may be transfers, promotions, demotions and retrenchment etc. Deficit can be met through new selection, promotions, demotions, transfers, and training etc.[15]

Significance of Human Resource Planning

The salient features of Human Resource Planning can be enumerated as follows:

(i) It provides information about the manner in which the existing personnel are deployed and the kind of skills required for different jobs.

(ii) It serves the purpose of a planning and control technique.

(iii) It assesses future accommodations requirements.

(iv) It anticipates redundancies and avoids unnecessary dismissals.

(v) It determines the recruitment level.

(vi) It gives an indication of the lead time available to select and retain the required additional manpower.[1]

(vii) It accurately estimates the number of personnel required.

(viii) It help utilising the existing manpower more productively in relation to the job requirements.

Need for Human Resource Planning

Human Resource Planning is a means of preparing for future contingencies, estimating the likelihood of their occurrence and determining what should and can be done, when, if, and as they arise. It is, in effect, a means of controlling and manipulating the future through minimizing uncertainty. Human Resource Planning requires foresight, determination and an awareness of what is happening and is likely to happen which will affect the life of the enterprise. This is a difficult task because of the nature of our changing circumstances.[17]

Human Resource Accounting (HRA)

The recent trend in Human Resource Planning and control emphasizes the relevance of human resources accounting for formulating an effective manpower plan. The efficiency of a plan is also measured on the 'cost control aspect' taken into account by the plan. The realm of Human Resource Planning is very wide, and 'manpower budget' is the pertinent section in it which takes care of the cost aspect of the plan. Though, at present, human resource accounting is not being incorporated into any of the published financial statements of companies, many managers have taken cognisance of HRA's potential as an aid to Human Resource Planning, especially in maintaining the manpower budget of an organisation.

Human resources accounting envisages capitalization of all expenses (not utilized within a financial year). The endeavour of a 'management' must be to have such a manpower budget which will have a balancing effect on attritional effects of manpower cost, and the appreciating effect of expansional costs of manpower. This is accomplished with the active aid of HRA as a tool.[18] Das[19] conceived the human resource accounting as the process of identifying, measuring and communicating informations necessary for Human Resource Planning and control. It is used as a tool for the acquision, training, development, allocation, maintenance and utilization of human resources in the organisation.

Manpower Plan

A manpower plan is a document on the basis of which the management of the organisation can strive to have the right number of people possessing the right type of skills at right times, in right jobs and at right places with a view to enabling the organization to achieve its short-term and long-term goals. The term 'Human Resource Planning' makes different sense to different people. To some, it is training and development of managers in the areas of decision-making, communications and human behaviour. To some other people, it is estimating the future manpower requirements in quantitative terms. The first group considers Human Resource Planning exclusively in qualitative terms, whereas the second group expresses it in mere numbers. It needs to be realized that without quantitative forecasts of future manpower requirements, the training and development programs are likely to be divorced from reality. An undue emphasis on numerical forecasts, on the other hand, may result in ignoring the qualities that need to be properly developed up to a desired level. What is essential is a suitable mix of both the approaches thereby producing an integrated Human Resource Planning process.

A manpower plan must be set of two plans namely manpower demand plan, and manpower supply plan.

Manpower demand plan should spell out the manpower requirements of the organisation. It should, in principle, have five dimension: (I) quantitative (ii) qualitative, (iii) temporal, (iv) locational,(v) Job-positional. In case of organisations having office(s) at one place only, the fourth dimension is redundant.

Manpower supply plan is a reflex action to the manpower demand plan. It tries to present a set of alternative solutions to the problem of mobilising human resource as posed by the manpower demand plan. According to sources of supply, it subdivided into two distinct plans namely, a plan for supply from internal sources and a plan for supply from external sources. Both these plans naturally have the five dimensions stated above for the manpower demand plan. Modes of supply in case of the first supply plan are lateral and vertical transfers within the organization and that for the second plan is recruitment on temporary or permanent basis.[20]

Objectives of a Manpower Plan

(a) To integrate the plan with the long-range and short-range corporate planning.

(b) To ensure the optimum use of the human resources currently employed.

(c) To provide for the future manpower needs of the enterprise in terms of skills, numbers and ages.

Tools and Techniques of Manpower Plan

In order to achieve these objectives, the following concrete action-plans are suggested:

(i) Determine manpower needs – draw up manning tables and need forecasts,

(ii) Formulate plans for job-rotation, promotions and transfers where warranted and possible,

(iii) Draw-up training needs, design, phase out and ensure timely conduct of the training programmes,

(iv) Determine the time-table for recruitments and the levels at which the intake should take place,

(v) Draw-up, in terms of (i) above, deployment or interchangeability plans for the existing and proposed manpower by trades, departments, units, so that imbalances are avoided,

(vi) Maintain a constant audit on the results achieved (or not achieved) and a control on costs.[21]

Human Resource Planning tends to start with management – down to first level supervision. More elaborate and advanced plans may involve the entire workforce, particularly in organizations such as railroads with strong unions, substantial skill and experience requirements at all levels, and labour redundency problems.

Plans are dependent on objectives and forecasts. These must be continually updated; consequently, the manpower plan must be continually examined inn the light of changing needs and circumstances. Some aspects may not change.

In initiating formal Human Resource Planning it is probably wisest to aim at three to five years, with the greatest emphasis being put on the initial one year period. The real time determinant will be the level of overall planning existing within the organization.

Human Resource Planning should be co-ordinated and implemented by a corporate staff responding directly to top management. There is as yet no established pattern as to what organizational unit the Manpower Planner should belong. In some instances he may be part of personnel; in others, corporate planning, and in still others the function has been combined with Organizational Planning.

The actual planning must be done throughout the company, the Manpower Planner will determine the kinds of information required; act as a catalyst in obtaining this information, collate, analyse and summarize it in total corporation terms, work with line management and the personnel Department in developing action programs, and then monitor these programs to ensure that objectives are met.[22]

Manpower programming permits, on a totally integrated basis, the design and implementation of action programs to assure that the manpower needs of the firm are met over time. These programs entail all of the traditional personnel functions, but the emphasis here is on the acquisition and development of manpower skills. Thus, the functions of employment (recruitment, selection and placement) and education and training receive prime consideration.

Changes in manpower programs will take the form expansion, adjustment, contraction, or a combination of these. A complete description of action programs to meet manpower requirements would be unrealistic since the possibilities are almost innumerable.

From the foregoing discussion, it may be concluded that human resource planning ensures adequate supply, proper quantity and quality as well as effective utilization of human resources. Human resource planning is needed for foreseeing the human resource requirements of tourism organization and supply of human resources. Manpower plans ensure a continuous supply of trained people as and when the need arises. Long-term planning is concerned with fulfilling future vacancies rather than matching the present incumbents to present jobs.

REFERENCES

1. E. Geisler (1967). *Human Resource Planning: An Emerging Staff Function*, A.M.A., New York, p.229.
2. Pattanayak, Biswajeeet (2005). *Human Resource Management*, Prentice Hall of India Private Limited, New Delhi, p. 45.
3. Stainer, G. (1981), *Human Resource Planning*, William Heinemann Ltd., London, p. 3.
4. Coleman, Bruce P. (1980). "An Integrated System of Human Resource Planning", *Business Horizon*, Vol. 13, No. 5, pp. 89-95.
5. Gardon McBeath (1979), *Organisational and Human Resource Planning*, Second Edition, Business Books Limited, London, p. 55.
6. Beach, Dale S., *Personnel Management of People at Work*, p. 411.
7. Wickstrom, W.S. (1981), *Human Resource Planning: Evolving Systems*, Report, No. 251, The Conference Board, New York, p. 2.
8. Velter, Eric W. (2003), *Human Resource Planning for High Talent Personnel*, p. 15.
9. Third Five Year Plan (1961-66), Government of India, Planning Commission, pp. 160-168.

10. http://www.buzzle.com/editorials/9-12-2004-59200.asp
11. Varma, M.K. Human Resource Planning: Conceptual Framework', *Indian Management*, (2002) New Delhi.
12. Mamoria, C.B. and Gankar S.V. (2002), *Personnel Management*, Himalaya Publishing House, Mumbai, p. 160.
13. Sikula, A.F. (2000), *Personnel Administration and Human Resource Planning*, John Wiley & Sons, New York, p. 148.
14. Cox, Ame (1968), 'Personnel Planning; Objectives and Methods – Presentation of Integrated System,' *Management International Review*, Vol. 8, No. 4-5, pp. 104-114.
15. Gupta, C.B. (2000), *Human Resource Management*, Sultan Chand and Sons, N. Delhi, pp. 2.11 – 2.15.
16. Arvind Chauhan and Vithalbhai Patel, (1980), 'Human Resource Planning', *Indian Management*, Vol. 19, No. 10, New Delhi, p. 37.
17. Johnston, C.P. and Meridith H.A. (Winter, 1968), 'Human Resource Planning – Strategy and Implications', *The Business Quarterly*, Volume 33, No. 4, pp. 65-75.
18. Bhat, V. Prasanna, 'Cost of 'Attrition' in Human Resource Planning and HRA,' *Indian Management*, New Delhi.
19. Das, S.K. (1989), 'Human Resource Accounting and Productivity', *Productivity*, Vol. 30, No. 3, p. 315.
20. Varde, S.D. (1972), 'Human Resource Planning At the Level of An Indian Commercial Bank', *Prajnan*, Bombay, Oct.-Dec., pp. 331-346.
21. Varma, M.K., 'Human Resource Planning: A Plan of Action', *Indian Management*, New Delhi.
22. Johnston, C.P. and H.A. Medith (Winter, 1968), 'Human Resource Planning Strategy and Implications', *The Business Quarterly*, Volume 33, No. 4, pp. 65-75.

4

Recruitment and Selection

In the light of the significance of human resource planning as traced out in the previous chapter, the present chapter is devoted to the actual practices of recruitment and selection of human force in the tourism sector in India.

Recruitment

Recruitment is the first step in the employment of labour. It is the method by means of which labour is brought into industry. It is a process of searching for prospective employees and stimulating and encouraging them to apply for a job in an organization. Recruitment means listing of a number of candidates for any job in the organization so as to select the best person from among them. Recruitment is a positive function.

Recruitment may be defined as an activity that brings the job-seekers and job-givers (employers) face to face with one another to achieve certain goals. Recruitment follows Human Resource Planning. Recruitment needs are of three types – planned, anticipated and unexpected. Planned needs arise from changes in organization and retirement policy. Resignations, deaths, accidents and illness give to unexpected needs. Anticipated needs refer to those movements in personnel which an organization can predict by studying trends in the internal and external environments.

Government today does not leave the business only to the private sector. Both the Central and the State governments are now directly engaged in setting up economic and industrial enterprises. The system of recruitment differs considerably from the public sector controlled organizations to the private sector organizations. The nature of management as such is bound to be different in various organizations. Size of the organization, employment conditions, past recruitment efforts, working conditions, salary and other benefits, level of seasonality, cultural, economical and legal factors etc. affect recruitment system. Image of the organization, unattractive job, internal organizational policy, government influences etc. are constraints of recruitment.

Selection

Selection is the process of choosing the most suitable persons out of all the applicants. In this process relevant information about applicants is collected through a series of steps so as to evaluate their suitability for the job to be filled. Selection is a process of matching the qualifications of applicants with the job requirements. It is a process of weeding out unsuitable candidates and finally identify the most suitable candidate. Selection divides all the applicants into two categories – (a) suitable, and (b) unsuitable. Selection may be described as a process of rejection because generally more candidates are turned away than are hired. Selection is different from recruitment. Recruitment technically precedes selection. Recruitment involves identifying the sources of manpower and stimulating them to apply for jobs in the organization. On the other hand, selection is the process of choosing the best out of those recruited. Recruitment is positive as it aims at increasing the number of applications for wider choice or for increasing the selection ratio. Selection is negative as it rejects a large number of applicants to identify the few who are suitable for the job. Recruitment involves prospecting or searching whereas selection involves comparison and choice of candidates. The purpose of selection is to pick up the right person for every job. Selection is an important function as no organization can achieve its goals without selecting the right people. Faulty selection leads to wastage of time and money and spoils the environment of an organization. Scientific selection and placement of personnel can go a longway in building up a stable work force. It helps to reduce absenteeism and labour turnover. Proper selection is helpful in increasing the efficiency and productivity of the enterprise.

Selection process begins after the organization has received desired number of applications through one or more sources of recruitment. It involves a careful screening and testing of applicants so as to select the best and the most suitable from among them. After evaluation of applicants through tests and interview, physical examinations, etc., the best among the applicant may be hired. As regards unskilled employees, the personnel department may itself appoint them, but for skilled and semi-skilled jobs, the selection is generally left to be made by the supervisor/foreman who had placed the requisition for employees.

The tourism industry in its truest sense is all about movement of people to different places and experiences. It makes the people who work in that industry restless by nature and this makes loyalty a very rare quality. The challenge for the industry is not to create loyalty but to attract people of a high quality, who can take on growth opportunities and challenges early on and who can maximize their potential even during a short tenure with the organization. This requires recruitment strategies and training policies, which are able to train the selected employees and make them multiskilled employees who meet the requirements of the tourism industry as far as possible, and have the right person, at the right time and at the right place.

Placement

Placement is the process of assigning a specific job to each one of the selected candidates. It involves assigning a specific rank and responsibility to an individual. It implies matching the requirements of a job with the qualifications of candidate. Placement is the determination of the job to which an accepted candidate is to be assigned, and his assignment to that job. It is a matching of what the supervisor has reason to think he can do with the job demands. It is a matching of what he imposes in strain, working conditions, and what he offers in the form of payroll, companionship with others, promotional possibilities, etc. Proper placement helps improve employee morale. It also helps reduce employee turnover, absenteeism and accident rates. If a candidate adjusts himself to the job and continues to perform as per expectations, it might mean that the candidate is properly placed. However, if the candidate has problems in adjusting himself to the job and he continues to perform below expectations, he might be misplaced. Supervisor/executives should review all such cases to find out cases of misplacement. Such candidates should be assigned some other more suitable jobs. Alternately they may be given further training to make them fit for the job.

Induction or Orientation

When a new employee joins an organization, he is completely a stranger to the people, work place and the work environment. Therefore, he is likely to feel insecure, shy and nervous. In the absence of information and support there is likely to be anxiety and fear in his mind. He may undergo reality shock caused by a gap between his expectations and the real situation. Induction or orientation can help overcome these problems. Once an employee is selected and place on an appropriate job, the process of familiarizing him with the job and the organization begins. This process is called induction or orientation.

Orientation or induction is the process of receiving and welcoming an employee when he first joins a company and giving him the basic information he needs to settle down quickly and happily and start work. The new employee is introduced to the job and the organization. The purpose of orientation is to make the new entrant feel at home and develop a sense of pride in the organization and commitment to the job. The newcomer is explained his duties and responsibilities, company policies and rules, and other relevant information to get acquainted and accommodated with the organization. Orientation is, therefore, the process of introduction, welcoming, acclimatization, acculturatisation and socialization.

HOTEL 'THE PARK', NEW DELHI: A CASE STUDY

Established in 1910, Apeejay Surrendra Group with multifarious operations in tea plantations, hotels and restaurants, shipping, real estate, construction, financial services and information technology, play a significant role in the development of trade and commerce in India. Strong commitment to traditional ethics and values, the team of professionals at the Apeejay Surrendra Group continues to nurture the growth and development of the organization.

The Park Hotels, are a collection of luxury boutique hotels in India. The Park Hotels commenced operations with the opening of 'The Park', Calcutta in 1967. Today, located in Bangalore, Chennai, Kolkata, New Delhi and Visakhapatnam, the hotels have achieved global standards of product quality and service excellence with 35 years of industry experience. A destination of choice for corporate and leisure travellers these hotels, due to their downtown location, give easy access to key commercial and entertainment districts. Here contemporary design is embellished with tradition; trendy and fun. F&B concepts create new entertainment options and intimate and personalized services create industry benchmarks. A newly formed division of the Apeejay Surrendra Hotels, Boutique Hotels India provides management and marketing expertise in the hospitality industry.

Designed around business and leisure travellers, 'The Park', New Delhi' is located in the heart of the city centre. 'The Park' touches to the 224 rooms and suites and bring out the best in luxury, style and comfort. The residence, a deluxe floor, is gorgeous with the latest amenities and a display of glassy artworks. Its business services are ideal for clients to host successful banquets and conferences.

Superior Room

The 188 luxurious rooms are elegantly decked up with art and provide electronic safes, minibars, Internet, voicemail and cable TV. Every room is designed with care, so as to fuse sophistication with all the comforts and conveniences of a modern lifestyle. Indulgences like herbal toiletries further add to the lavishness.

Accommodation

Divided into rooms and luxuriant suites, which are meticulously furnished, the residence is symbolic of luxury. All the rooms come along with contemporary business necessities, in-room fax machines, dual-line-hands, free telephones and the Internet. To make the guests really comfortable, 'The Park' New Delhi also provides a private Jacuzzi and a personal valet. The Residence Lounge is ideal for private meetings, complimentary cocktails and hearty breakfasts.

There are around one thousand employees from top to bottom. To coordinate the working of the employees and to give best of the services to its large number of clients, it is necessary to have a sound Human Resource Planning Requirement and Selection policy. For this, a highly qualified officer is appointed who is designated as Human Resource Manager.

Hotel 'The Park', New Delhi, has planned for computerization of nearly 50 per cent of the covered area of the hotel. It has taken care of all resources in the computerization plan including human resources.

TABLE 4.1

Inventory of Human Resources and Future Requirements of Hotel 'The Park', New Delhi (as on 31.12.2007)

Category of Human Resources	*Present Inventory*	*Requirements after computerization*	*Surplus*
Managers (Food and Beverage)	15	8	7
Manager (Lobby)	2	2	0
Captains	20	8	12
Waiters	30	10	20
Engineers (Civil)	5	1	4
Total	72	29	43

Source: As per Records of Hotel 'The Park', New Delhi.

The human resource planners suggested the redeployment of managers (accommodation) in their newly started hotel 'The Park' Visakhapatnam and retrench surplus employee of all other categories. They also recommended to the management that there was no need for further recruitment or for any other action plan.

Remarkably, the computerization was over by the end of 2004. When the management wanted to start the hotel on the newly computerized process, it was shocked to note that many employees in the accommodation department were suitable to the new jobs and the information supplied by the human resource planners in this regard did not match with reality. The best solution was to formulate job specifications for the Graduate in hotel management required for modernization and advertise the posts for exform recruitment and simultaneously implement plan including splitting the plan into short and medium term, management principle used and conclusions should be written by the managers.

Steps in Recruitment Process

The recruitment process consists of the following steps:

1. Recruitment process generally begins when the personnel department receives requisitions for recruitment from any department of the hotel. The personnel requisitions contain details about the position to be filled, number of persons to be recruited the duties to be performed, qualifications required from the candidate, terms and conditions of employment and the time by which the persons should be available for appointment etc.
2. Locating and developing the sources of required number and type of employees.
3. Identifying the prospective employees with required characteristics.
4. Communicating the information about the organization, the job and the terms and conditions of service.
5. Encouraging the identified candidates to apply for jobs in the organization.
6. Evaluating the effectiveness of recruitment process.

Recruitment Policy

Recruitment policy of 'The Park' New Delhi specifies the objectives of recruitment and provide framework for the implementation of the recruitment programme. It involves commitment to principles such as enriching the organisation's human resources by filling vacancies with the best qualified people, attitudes towards recruitment minority groups, women, friends and relatives of press employees, and promotion from within. Recruitment policy is based on the recognition that it is hard to find qualified executives. The recruitment policy involves the employer's commitment to such general principles as

(a) To find and employ the best qualified persons for each job.

(b) To retain the most promising of those hired.

(c) To offer promising opportunities for life time working careers;

(d) To provide facilities and opportunities for personal growth on the job.

The Park have a planned and systematic recruitment policy to minimize disruption of work due to changes in employees and to secure equitable distribution of employment opportunities. A well-considered and pre-planned recruitment policy based on the goals, needs and environment of the organization will surely avoid hasty or ill-conceived decisions and help to man the organization with the right kind of personnel.

Sources of Recruitment

Various sources of recruitment for the Park Hotel may be classified into broad categories, namely internal sources and external sources.

Internal Sources: Internal sources consists of the following:

(a) Present employees – permanent, temporary and causal employees already on the pay of the organization are a good source. Vacancies may filled up from such employees through promotions, transfers, upgrading and even domotions. Transfer implies shifting of an employee from one job to another without any major change in the status and responsibilities of the employee.

(b) Retired and retrenched employees who want to return to the company may be rehired.

(c) Dependents and relatives of deceased and disabled employees.

External Sources: External sources of recruitment are as follows:

(a) Educational and Training Institutions: Various institutes like IIMs, Hotel Management Institutes, SITA Academy etc. are a good source for recruiting well qualified executives, managers, hoteliers etc. They provide facilities for a campus interviews and placement. Good institutions have placement cells/officers to serve as liaison between the employers and the students. This source is known as campus recruitment.

(b) Recruitment Agencies: Several private consultancy firms e.g. A.F. Furguson Associates, Price Waterhouse, ABC consultants, etc. perform recruitment function on behalf of client companies by charging fee. These agencies are particularly suitable for recruitment of executives and specialists. They perform all the functions of recruitment and selection so that the client is relieved of this burden. But the cost of recruitment through these agencies is quite high.

(c) Employment Exchange: Public employment exchanges set up by Govt. of India throughout the country. These exchanges provide information about job vacancies to the jobseekers and help employers identifying suitable candidates. They contain a data bank of candidates for different types of jobs. Whenever they get requisition/ notice from employers the concerned candidate are informed.

(d) Causal Callers: Due to widespread unemployment in the country many jobseekers visit the offices of well known companies on their own. Such callers are generally considered a nuisance to the daily work routine of the enterprise. But a waiting list of such unsolicited visitors can be prepared to the temporary and lower level jobs. It is a very inexpensive source of recruitment.

(e) Labour Contractors: Manual workers can be recruited through contractors who maintain close links with the sources of such workers. This source is often used to recruit labour for construction jobs.

(f) Similar Organisations: Experienced employees can be recruited offering better benefits to the people working in similar organization. New established organizations of well known business houses often lure experienced executives and technical experts from the public sector.

(g) Press Advertisement: Conventionally, advertisement in newspapers and journals is a widely used source of recruitment. The advantage of this method is that it has a very wide reach. One advertisement in a leading daily can cover millions of persons throughout the country. Cost per person is very low. This method can be used for clerical, technical and managerial jobs.

Methods of Recruitment

Various methods are employed by 'The Park Hotel', New Delhi for recruitment of employees which may be classified into the following categories:

1. *Direct Methods:* Under direct recruitment scouting, employee contacts, manned exhibits and waiting lists are used. In scouting, representative of the organisation are sent to educational and training institutions. Their travelling recruiters exchange information with the students, clarify their doubts, stimulate them to apply for jobs, conduct campus interviews and show list of candidates for further screening.

2. *Indirect Methods:* Advertisement in newspapers, journals, on the radio and television are used to publicise vacancies. A well thought out and clear advertisement enables candidates to assess their suitability so that only those possessing the requisite qualifications will apply. This method is appropriate when the organization wants to reach out to a large target group scattered geographically.
3. *Third Party Methods:* Various agencies can be used to recruit personnel. Public employment exchanges, management consulting firms, professional societies, temporary help societies, trade unions, labour contractors and the main agencies. In addition, friends and relatives of existing staff and deputation method can also be used.

The Park Hotel generally go for direct methods but do not stick to that only. It also used indirect methods and third party methods to make best use of resources.

Selection Procedure at 'The Park'

The selection procedure consists of a series of steps. At each stage facts may come to light which may lead to the rejection of the applicant. It is a series of successive hurdles or barriers which an applicant must cross. These hurdles or screens are designed to eliminate an unqualified candidate at any point in the selection process.

The steps involved in employee's selection at The Park Hotel may be described as under:

1. *Preliminary Interview:* First of all, initial screening is done to weed out totally undesirable/unqualified candidates at the outset. Preliminary interview is essentially a sorting process in which prospective candidates age given the necessary information about the nature of the job and the organization, necessary information is also elicited from the candidates about the education, skills, experience, salary expected, etc. If the candidate is form suitable, he is selected for further screening.

2. *Selection Test:* Psychological tests are also done in employee selection. A test is a sample of some aspect of an individual's attitudes, behaviour and performance. It also provides a systematic basis for comparing the behaviour, performance and attitudes of two or more persons. Tests are based on the assumption that individuals differ in their job related traits which can be measured. Tests help to reduce bias in selection by serving as supplementary screening device. Tests are helpful in better matching of candidate and the job. Tests may also reveal qualifications which remain covered in application form and interview.
3. *Employment Interview:* An interview is a conversation between two persons. In selection it involves a personal, observational and face to face appraisal of candidates for employment. Interview is an essential element of selection and no selection process is complete without one or more personal interviews. The information collected through application and test are cross-checked in the interview.
4. *Reference Checks:* The applicant is asked to mention in his application form the names and addresses of two or three persons who know him well. These may be his previous employers, heads of educational institutions or public figures. The organization contacts them by mail or telephone. They are requested to provide their frank opinion about the candidate without incurring any liability. They are assured that all information supplied will be kept confidential. The opinion of referees can be useful in judging the future behaviour and performance of a candidate. But it is not advisable to rely exclusively on the referees because they are generally biased in favour of the candidate.
5. *Final Approval:* In 'The Park' Hotel selection process is carried out by the human resource department. The decisions of this department are recommendatory. The

candidates short listed by the department are finally approved by the executives of the concerned department/ units. Employment is offered in the form of an appointment letter mentioning the post, the rank, the salary grade, the date by which the candidate should join and other terms and conditions in brief. Appointment is generally made on a probation of one or two years. After satisfactory performance during this period the candidate is usually confirmed on the job on permanent basis or regularized.

Hotel 'The Park' searches at IIMs and other frontline business schools such as reputed Institutes of Hotel Management, Catering and Nutrition of India located in different parts of the country for its recruitment. But, this is a cumbersome exercise. So it concentrate on the B-schools/Institutes of Hotel Management, Catering and Nutrition where curricula and specialization match with the hotel's needs. It evaluates the education standards at all leading B-school and Institute of Hotel Management, Catering and Nutrition including the quality of classroom education, strengths of faculty and the support systems such as libraries, and computerized referencing. It also scans the entrance test marks of each B-school/Institute of Hotel Management, Catering and Nutrition to ensure that students being admitted – whom it will target later – are intellectually superior. Only the schools that fit its stringent standards remain on its list which is reviewed every year.

Field survey shows that members of most effective recruitment team should be between 30 and 45 years, be line managers rather than general managers and have thorough knowledge of the hotel and the job. The hotel should include an alumni from the B-school/Institute of Hotel Management, Catering and Nutrition from which it is hiring to get a favourable reference. The composition of the team reflects how seriously the campus recruitment is taken. B-school graduates are more interested in the work culture of the hotel – level of responsibility, degree of autonomy, extent of elbow room with potential and scope of learning.

On the whole The Park Hotels have thousands of employees. The group has very effective & efficient Human Resource Policies and Practices, which drags it to the path of progress by leaps and bounds.

Conclusion

Recruitment is concerned with developing suitable techniques for attracting more and more candidates. Recruitment is a linkage activity bringing together those with jobs and those seeking jobs. The recruitment policy is concerned with quantity and qualifications of manpower. Economic conditions of a country influence the recruitment process in all the tourism organizations. The management has to consider several varieties in deciding on the extent to which they will depend on internal and external sources of recruitment, internal sources often lead to inbreeding.

Selection is the process of choosing candidates for employment. Selection procedure may be compared to a series of barriers which an applicant is required to cross before he is finally selected. The success of tourism industry depends upon the quality of personnel selected for the jobs.

The succeeding chapter deals with training and development in tourism sector which includes objectives, methods, various training programmes in the field of Tourism, Hotel Management, Catering and Nutrition.

5

Training and Development

The previous chapter discussed the recruitment and selection of personnel for the Indian tourism sector. The process has analysed with reference to the case study of Hotel 'The Park', New Delhi. Training and Development of personnel is another important aspect of human resource planning and development. The present chapter deals with this aspect of human resource planning in Indian tourism sector.

Training is a necessity and not a luxury. Many tourism industries spend huge amounts on training as it is generally felt that it motivates employees to put hard work. If employees understand job well, their morale increases and there is also a sense of recognition among the employees that they are the valued members of the enterprise.

The term 'training' refers to a systematic procedure for transferring technical know-how to the employees so as to increase their knowledge and skills for doing particular jobs. "Training is the act of increasing the knowledge and skills of an employee for doing a particular job".[1] It involves the development of skills that are usually necessary to perform a specific job. Its purpose is to achieve a change in the behaviour of those trained and to enable them to do their jobs better.

Training is the teaching of vocational or practical aspect and relates to specific useful skills. It forms the core of apprenticeships and provides the backbone of content at technical colleges or polytechnics. Today it is often referred to as professional development .

Training is defined as learning practically in order to improve performance on the present job. A person's performance is improved by showing her how to master a new or established technology. The technology may be a piece of heavy machinery, a computer, a procedure for creating a product, or a method of providing a service.[2]

Every tourism organization is to arrange for systematic training of its workforce. If no systematic training is organized by the organization, the workers will try to train themselves by trial and error or by observing others. But this process will take a lot of time and will result in higher costs of training. Moreover, the workers may not be able to learn the best operating methods. Training is important not only from the point of view of the tourism organization, but also for the employee. Training is valuable to the employees because it will give them greater job security and an opportunity for advancement. A skill acquired through training is an asset for both the organization and the employee. It can be taken away only by the complete elimination of the need for that skill because of rapid technological changes.

Training, Development and Education

HRD programmes are divided into three main categories: Training, Development and Education. Although some organizations lump all learning under "Training" or "Training and Development", dividing it into three distinct categories that makes the desired goals and objects more meaningful and precise.

Training helps in the acquisition of technology which permits employees to perform their present job to standards. It improves human performance on the job the employee is presently doing or is being hired to do.

Education, on the other hand, is training people to do a different job. It is often given to people who have been identified as being promotable, being considered for a new job either lateral or upwards, or to increase their potentials. Unlike training, which can be fully evaluated immediately upon the learners returning to work, education can only be completely evaluated when the learners move on to their future jobs or tasks.

Development is training people to acquire new horizons, technologies, or viewpoints. It enables leaders to guide their organizations onto new expectations by being proactive rather than reactive. It enables workers to create better products, faster services, and more competitive organizations. It is learning for growth of the individual, but not related to a specific present or future job. Unlike training and education, which can be completely evaluated, development cannot always be fully evaluated.

Development involves changes in an organism that are systematic, organized, and successive and are thought to serve an adaptive function.[3]

Further, development refers to the progress that the individual makes in learning whereas training refers to the programmes developed to facilitate this learning process. Training and Management Development for productivity is concerned with the acquisition or development of those knowledges, skills, techniques, attitudes and experiences which enable an individual to make his most effective contribution to the combined effort of the team of which he is a member.

In fact, training and development are different from each other on the following five important counts :

(a) Training is meant for operatives, whereas development is meant for executives.

(b) The aim of training is to develop some specific skill in an individual, while the aim of development is to develop the total personality of the individual.

(c) Training is a one-shot affair but development is a continuous process.

(d) The initiative for training comes from management. The initiative for development comes from the individual himself. Training is mostly the result of some outside motivation. Development is the result of internal motivation.

(e) Training is mostly a preparation to meet an individual's present needs. It can thus be seen as a reactive process. On the other hand, development is the preparation to meet an individual's future needs. It is thus largely a proactive process.[4]

Objectives of Training and Development

Training and development together have the following common objectives :

- To improve the employee's knowledge and skills.
- To bring about necessary attitudinal changes.
- To develop employees for shouldering higher responsibilities.
- To be a source of self-development for employees.
- To improve organizational effectiveness and climate.
- To provide a rich learning experience to manage the organization.
- To create suitable conditions and climate in the growth process of the organisation.
- To prevent managerial obsolescence.
- To tackle the labour problems in the organisation with tact; and
- To bring about change in the knowledge, attitude, behaviour and performance of the managerial personnel.

Training and Development Programmes are designed for imparting knowledge and infuse attitudinal change to arouse creativity and innovative qualities for changing the 'Raw' human resource which can make only a limited contribution into a dynamic sagacious force to effectively manage and realize the organisational objective. A training and development programme should not be inculcated only to create specific skills with the help of requisite knowledge and attitude to meet the need or maintain the existing performance level but it should also involve professional growth, management effectiveness and thereby organizational development. The TDP is a vital organ for management control as on one hand it reduces the cost by reducing accidents and wastages and on the other, it increases the quantity and quality of the product, thus enhancing both individual and organisational productivity. To meet the challenges of the modern industrial world it is imperative that managers must develop creativity, tenacity and competence. Thus, the role of TDP to nourish and sharpen the talent for fruitful and purposeful action.

The Training and Development programmes cover all the facets of an industrial endeavour right from managing people, job and other social and legal responsibilities. Management of men and machine for enhancing the quality and quantity of the products, reduction in the cost of investment and human resource management are other ingredients of TDP.

The role of Training and Development programmes is most essential as it helps not only in 'managing others', but in 'managing self' and it inculcates among the participants a feeling to aspire for higher and higher excellence and effectiveness and thereby increased productivity.[5]

Productivity of tourism organization is directly related to the managerial effectiveness. It depends directly on how well the managers are trained to plan and execute tourism organizational plans. Identifying and evaluating the factors which contribute to managerial effectiveness and making an earnest effort to develop these skills are of critical importance. An effective team of managers is of paramount importance to the survival of the organization.

Today, Training and Management Development is not a choice left to the goodwill of the top management, neither a luxury of profitable corporation nor a fringe benefit of large organizations. It is a requirement of the economic system, a process imposed on the company as a result of organizational growth, changing technology, and a changing competitive environment in its broadest sense. A systematic training and management development is one of the primary tasks of an organization for its own survival in a rapidly changing environment.

An effective management recognizes that training and development is an on going and continuous process, not a 'one shot' activity. New problems, new procedures and equipments, new knowledge and new jobs are constantly creating the need for training and development. On justification for the investment of time, money, or any other resources in training and development activities is that, it can contribute to the productivity and profitability of the enterprise. Training activities, properly planned, conducted and evaluated, help to raise the productivity of the enterprise through the more effective use of human resources.[6]

Methods of Training

A number of methods of training in industrial organizations are in vogue. The various methods of training may be mentioned here as under:

1. On the job-training;
2. Off the job-training;
3. Management Development
4. Apprenticeship Training

There are also some other important methods being followed in state, regional and national level training institutes of tourism. They are :

- Lecture method;
- Statement discussion;
- Discussion method;
- Syndicate method;
- Seminars;
- Conference;
- Symposium;
- Role playing;
- Business games;

- T-group training;
- Case studies method;
- Programme Instructions;
- Web-based training;
- Computer based training;
- Using CD-ROMs for training;

Now-a-days, Total Quality Management (TQM) is not a choice. It is an imperative for survival, as otherwise. Indian organizations that do not do the right things at the right time and right things the first time, will be totally wiped out. So, many Indian organizations have started taking training for TQM, in a very serious way.

Quality is an essential ingredient for organization success. The quality of training, education, research, extension service to the trainees and farming community must improve for the success of the "Quality Movement" in our country. TQM is people-oriented rather than based on systems and techniques, and it is they (people) who make TQM a reality and a success. TQM cannot be implemented similar to adoption of agricultural production technology – it must be practiced, lived and nurtured. Therefore, it is important to ensure that organizational culture and values are conducive to TQM. Without the total commitment of the Head of the Institution and his/her immediate colleagues, nothing much will happen and anything that does will not be permanent. They must take personal charge and exercise forceful and personal leadership.

TQM is based on fairness. It requires the organizations to satisfy its customer, and to be honest with its people. Every organization, like every human, has moral feelings. Before a TQM programme starts, the administrators should carry out an ethics, audit draw up an ethics policy. The ethics audit should cover relationships between faculty and students, faculty and administration, researcher and farmers, relevance of curriculum and its ground realities, organisation's attitude etc. TQM means thinking about quality in terms of all functions of the enterprise and is a start-to-finish process that integrates interrelated functions at all levels. It is a systems approach that considers every interaction between the various elements of the organization. Thus, the overall effectiveness of the system is higher than the sum of the individual outputs from the subsystems include are the organizational functions in the life cycle of a product, such as design, planning, production, distribution and field service.[7]

Training Programmes in the Field of Tourism, Hotel Management, Catering and Nutrition

Training programme in the field of Hotel Management, Catering and Nutrition were initiated by Government of India in the year 1952 under the Department of Food, Ministry of Agriculture. Initially, four Institutes of Hotel Management, Catering Technology and Applied Nutrition were set up at New Delhi, Mumbai, Chennai and Kolkata for imparting training in hospitality. Twelve food Craft Institutes were also set up later at different places in the country. Consequent upon transfer of the programme to the Ministry of Tourism in October 1982, format of the various training programmes was re-oriented and remodeled keeping in view the work needs of the country's fast expanding accommodation and catering industry. Later on, Ministry of Tourism also established the National Council for Hotel Management and Catering Technology (NCHMCT) in the year 1982. The main objectives for setting up the Council at the apex level were :

(a) To advise the Government on co-ordinated development of hotel management and catering education.

(b) To implement international development in the area of human resource development for the hospitality sector.

(c) To affiliate institutes and prescribe courses of study and instructions leading to examinations conducted by it.

(d) To standardize courses and infrastructure requirements for institutes imparting education and training in hospitality management.

(e) To prescribe educational and other qualifications,

experience, etc. for members of staff in the affiliated institutes and organize faculty development programme.

(f) To grant affiliation to Institutes at the national level.

(g) To award Certificates and Diplomas.

As a result of fast expansion and modernization of the country's hospitality industry, hotel management and catering education programmes gained tremendous popularity. Now, courses offered by the National Council are of international standard which have been recognized by the hospitality industry. At present, there are 24 Institutes of Hotel Management and 6 Food Craft Institutes following National Council's course curriculum. National Council has consistently worked on augmentation of training capacity in the different Institutes of Hotel Management. Thus, there has been a constant increase in the intake in the first year of the 3-year Degree Programme. Compared to intake of 2525 in year 2002, the intake in year 2003 increased to 2760.[8]

National Council for Hotel Management and Catering Technology (NCHMCT)

The Council has emerged as the apex formation for regulating hospitality studies through 31 Institutes that are affiliated with the National Council. The Council offers several different streams of education and training. The Council also regulates admissions to the 3-Year Degree Programme in Hospitality and Hotel Administration for all its affiliated Institutes of Hotel Management.

National Council conducted 2003 annual examination for 9251 candidates for the eleven courses that it offers through 24 Institutes of Hotel Management and 6 Food Craft Institutes. Female candidates numbering 1401 have taken these examination registering 15.14% as average percentage of female candidates in all the courses. In case of P.G. course in Dietetics and Hospital Food Service, it is cent percent for female students.

National Council (NCHMCT) and Indira Gandhi National Open University (IGNOU) have launched the M.Sc. programme in Hospitality Administration from November 2003 at the Institute of Hotel Management, Pusa, New Delhi, and at the Institute of Hotel Management, Bangalore.

TABLE 5.1

Course-wise Share of Female Candidates

Course/Year	*Appeared*	*Female*	*Percentage*
1st Year of 3-Year Degree	2798	425	15.18
2nd Year of 3-Year Degree	2238	376	16.80
3rd Year of 3-Year Degree	2100	362	17.23
P.G.A.O.	261	40	15.32
P.G.D.H.F.S.	77	77	100.00
Craft Food Production	547	25	4.57
Craft F&B Service	359	07	1.95
Craft Hotel & Catering Management	50	02	4.00
Diploma in Food Production	286	30	10.48
Diploma in F&B Service	246	09	3.65
Diploma in Front Office Operation	112	24	21.42
Diploma in House-keeping	86	12	13.95
Diploma in Bakery & Confectionery	91	12	13.18
Total	9251	1401	15.14

Source: Annual Report (2006-07), India Tourism, Government of India, p. 53.

Development of HRD Infrastructure for Training in Hospitality Education Sector

The Government has sanctioned an Institute of Hotel Management (IHM) in the State of Haryana at Kurukshetra. The work has been entrusted to CPWD and is in progress. The Government has also sanctioned an Institute of Hotel Management for the State of Utrtaranchal at Dehradun. The Hon'ble Minister for Tourism and Culture has since laid the foundation stone for the new complex. This project is likely to be ready soon which will be responsible to cater to hospitality human resource requirements of the State of Uttaranchal. The other two Hotel Management Institutes have been earmarked for the States of Chhattisgarh and Jharkhand.

TABLE 5.2

Status of Building Projects of the Institutes of Hotel Management (IHMs) as on 31.03.2006

Name of the Project	*Year of Sanction*	*Amount sanctioned (Rs. in lacs)*	*Amount re-lease so far (Rs. in lacs)*
IHM-Ahmedabad	1991 Project revised in 1999-2000	799.45	342.00
IHM-Bangalore Executive Development Centre (EDC)	1999-2000	495.00 (G.O.I. share 395.00 and 100.00 to be raised by IHM)	150.00
IHM-Bangalore Girls Hostel	2003-2004	215.00	80.00
IHM-Kolkata	1998-1999	324.00	324.00
IHM-Chennai	2000-2001	465.41	284.00
IHM-Goa	1999-2000 Revised in 2002	310.37	310.37
IHM-Guwahati	1998-1999 Revised in 2002	1280.50	701.83
IHM-Gwalior	2000-2001	728.05	513.97
IHM-Patna	1998-1999	1024.35 G.O.I. contri-bution share 764.04	758.33
IHM-Srinagar	1986 Revised in 1999-2000	806.00	250.00
IHM-Simla	1999-2000	941.20	700.00
IHM-Shillong	1998-99	1324.00	400.00
Headquarters of NCHMCT at NOIDA	2002-2003	1051.11 including land cost of 371.60	621.50
IHM-Kurukshetra, Haryana	2003 The proposal submitted by CPWD involves an estimated cost of Rs. 9.77 crores	977.00	150.50
IHM-Dehradun, Uttarakhand	2003 CPWD, Dehra-dun has furnished pre-liminary Estimate of Rs. 635.00 lakhs	635.00	75.00
State IHM-Sikkim at Rumtek	2003-2004	650.00	400.00

Source: Annual Report, Ministry of Tourism, Government of India, 2003-04, pp. 60-61.

The Department of Tourism has approved the proposal for up-gradation of the State Institute of Hotel Managemnt, Sikkim at a cost of Rs. 650.00 lakhs. The Institute offers 3-Year Programme in Hotel Management and shall play a vital role in imparting Hospitality Education and provide the required manpower in the Hospitality Industry not only for the State of Sikkim but also for the entire North-Eastern region.

Institute of Hotel Management, Catering Technology and Applied Nutrition – Ahmedabad

Institute of Hotel Management, Ahmedabad was established during 1972 and thereafter upgraded from Craft level to Management level during 1984. So far, around 1250 craft trainees and almost equal number of diploma level students have been trained.

With due transformation, the 3-Year Diploma has been upgraded to the level of Degree Programme. Under the Bachelor of Science (B.Sc.) in Hospitality and Hotel Administration, the intake capacity is 120 students and additionally other short-term courses are also conducted by the Institute.

Institute of Hotel Management, Catering Technology and Applied Nutrition – Bangalore

Institute of Hotel Management, Bangalore which was offering a Diploma in Hotel Management till 2001, is now offering a B.Sc. Degree in Hotel & Hospitality Administration in collaboration with IGNOU, from the year 2002. The Institute, in keeping with its previous record, has an enviable placement record of 100% for its final year batch of 2002-2003.

Institute of Hotel Management, Catering Technology and Applied Nutrition – Bhopal

Institute of Hotel Management, Bhopal was upgraded from craft Level Institute to Management Level Institute in the year 1986. The Institute has hostel facility with accommodation for 250 boys and 102 girls. The Institute at present offers 3-Year Degree Programme in Hotel Management with an intake of 180 students. It also offers Post Graduate Diploma in Accommodation

Operation, Post Graduate Diploma in Dietetics & Hospitality Food Service, Craftsmanship course in Food Production with an intake of 40 students in each.

Institute of Hotel Management, Catering Technology & Applied Nutrition – Bhubaneswar

Institute of Hotel Management Catering technology & Applied Nutrition, Bhubaneswar, was established as Food Craft Institute in the year 1973 and upgraded by Government of India to Diploma level in 1984. The Institute has acquired infrastructure to train over 500 students in each year. The courses offered by this Institute are : 3-Year B.Sc. Programme in Hospitality & Hotel Administration; Post Graduate Diploma in Accommodation Operation & Management; Craftsmanship Course in Food Production and Craftsmanship course in Food & Beverage Service.

Dr. Ambedkar Institute of Hotel Management, Catering & Nutrition – Chandigarh

The Institute was set-up in the year 1990. It is situated on a plot measuring 4.63 acres among lush green surroundings of the "City Beautiful" designed by the French Architect "Le Curbusier". At present, Institute offers Bachelor of Science programme in Hospitality and Hotel Administration with an intake of 150 students. The Institute being a professional and vocational training Institute trains and grooms highly motivated youth of India for gainful employment in fast developing hospitality industry of the country and also ensures professionalism at all levels, which includes hotels, motels, restaurants, tourist resorts, industrial canteens, consultancy firms, marketing and lecturers in hospitality management institutes, etc.

Institute of Hotel Management, Catering Technology and Applied Nutrition – Chennai

Institute of Hotel Management, Chennai was established by Government of India in the year 1963. In its own campus, the Institute has the main Institute Building and Hostel for boys and girls and the additional building is presently under construction.

The Institute offers 3 year Degree Programme in Hotel Management, Post Graduate Diploma in Accommodation Operation & Management, Post Graduate Diploma in dietetics and Hospital Food Service, Diploma in Food Production, Diploma in Bakery & confectionery, Diploma in Front Office Operation, Craft Course in Food Production, Craft course in Food & Beverage Service, and Certificate course in Hotel & Catering Management. The Institute has over 615 students on its roll.

Institute of Hotel Management, Catering and Nutrition–PUSA, New Delhi

Institute of Hotel Management, Catering & Nutrition, New Delhi popularly known as Pusa Institute was established by Central Government as the premier Institute in the country in 1962. With a modest initial intake of 10 students, the Institute at present has 570 students on its roll undergoing six hospitality-training programmes. The courses that it offers include popular 3-Year Degree Programme in Hotel Managemnt & Catering Technology, Post Graduate Diploma in Dietetics and Hospital Food Service, Craft course in Food Production. Diploma programmes in Food & Beverage Service and Bakery & confectionery Arts with an intake of 30 students in each.

Institute of Hotel Management, Catering Technology and Applied Nutrition – Goa

Institute of Hotel Management, Goa was upgraded to Management level Institute in the year 1984. The Institute provides hostel facility for boys and girls. The Institute is committed to achieving perfection in every aspect of hospitality, giving world class training to the students, through experienced faculty and contemporary equipment and facilities comparable with the best in the world.

The Institute offers 3-Year B.Sc. Degree course in Hospitality and Hotel Administration with an annual intake of 150 students. The Institute also offers Craft Courses in (i) Food Production and Patisserie and (ii) Food and Beverage Service.

Institute of Hotel Management, Catering Technology and applied Nutrition – Gurdaspur

Institute of Hotel Management, Catering and Nutrition, Gurdaspur is an autonomous body, which has been sponsored by the Ministry of Tourism, Government of India set up in the year 1994 and registered as Society under Punjab Society Act.

The Institute offers regular whole-time-3-Year Bachelor Degree in Hotel Management, Catering and Nutrition having an annual intake of 120. The Institute is affiliated to the National Council for Hotel Management and Catering Technology (An Apex body under Ministry of Tourism), New Delhi. The students are admitted to the course in this Institute by National Council for Hotel Management and Catering Technology, New Delhi through a joint entrance examination.

Institute of Hotel Management, Catering Technology & Applied Nutrition – Guwahati

Institute of Hotel Management, Catering Technology and Applied Nutrition, Guwahati was upgraded from Food Craft Institute to its present status w.e.f April 1995. This Institute in Guwahati is the pioneer for the entire North Eastern Region. At present, the Institute is offering 3-Year B.Sc. programme in Hospitality and Hotel Administration, P.G. Diploma in Accommodation Operation & Management (1½-Year Programme) and Craftsmanship Course in Food Production (1½-Year Programme).

Institute of Hotel Management, Catering Technology and Applied Nutrition, Gwalior

Institute of Hotel Management, Gwalior started as a Food Craft Institute in 1986, was jointly sponsored by Government of India and Government of Madhya Pradesh. Subsequently in 1992 it was upgraded to IHM level. The campus is located at Maharajpura in MP state. The students of the Institute are making a mark for themselves and substantially enhancing the brand equity of their alma mater, 77 students appeared in the final examination of the 3-Year Programme of 2002-2003, registering a pass percentage of 100%. Subsequently, 95% of the students found suitable placement through the campus recruitment/selection by the leading hotels and other service organizations.

The Institute runs courses aiming to benefit especially the local student community. It has also launched awareness-cum-training drive among the local hotel personnel, travel and tour operators and employees of the Archaeological Survey of India. The purpose is to give filling to the tourism activities in and around the City of the Gwalior. Under the Scheme of Capacity Building for Service Providers, the Institute has also initiated training programme to educate the local restaurant and "Dahaba" owners on aspects such as hygiene, courtesy and communication skills.

Institute of Hotel Management, Catering Technology and Applied Nutrition – Hyderabad

Institute of Hotel Management, Hyderabad was upgraded from Food Craft level of Managemnt level in the year 1984. The campus covers an area of 1.60 acres wherein the Institute building, hostels for 72 boys and 30 girls and staff quarters for two Wardens are located. The Institute, at present, offers 3-Year B.Sc. programme in Hospitality and Hotel Administration with an intake of 150 students. It also offers Post Graduate Diploma in Accommodation Operation and Management and Craft Course in Food production and Craft Course in Food & Beverage Service with respect intake of 20 and 50 students. The Institute has facilities for Badminton, Volley Ball, Tennis and other indoor and outdoor games.

Institute of Hotel Management, Catering Technology & Applied Nutrition – Jaipur

Institute of Hotel Management, Jaipur is upgraded from Food Craft Institute level to Management level in the year 1989. Its campus is located on a 2.5 acre plot where, besides state-of-the-art Institute building, it also houses hostel for 120 boys and 30 girls. Staff quarters are also located adjacent to its premises on a separate 1.5 acres plot. The Institute, at present, offers 3

Year Degree Programme in Hospitality & Hotel Administration. In annual examination for the third year of 3-Year Degree Programme, 95 students out of 96 successfully passed the course, registering a pass percentage of 98.96 while 41 students found placement in the industry through campus recruitment; the remaining have also managed suitable placements through other recruitment agencies.

Institute of Hotel Management, Catering Technology and Applied Nutrition – Kolkata

Institute of Hotel Management, Kolkata was established in the year 1963. It is housed on a 2.57-acre plot of land, which includes Institute building, hostels for 16y4 boys and 42 girls besides limited accommodation for staff in the campus. The Institute, at present offers 3-Year Degree Programme in Hotel Management with an annual intake of 200 students. It also offer studies in post Graduate Diploma in Accommodation Operation besides in the new campus. The Institute, at present, offers 3-Year Degree Programme in Hotel Management with an intake of 75 students and, in addition, the Institute also runs 1½-Year Diploma in Food Production with an intake of 20 students. Having secured 100% results in the final examination 2003, 90% of the passed out students were employed at different outlets.

Institute of Hotel Management - Shillong

Institute of Hotel Management, Shillong, is now in its second academic year of operation with its first batch of students having already proceeded for their stipulated Industrial Training at various leading hotels across the country. The second batch of students has also commenced their first year academic session of 2003-2004. The first ever National Council Examination results obtained by the IHM Shillong in its first academic year have been very encouraging with the total promoted percentage being 94.7%.

Institute of Hotel Management, Catering Technology & Applied Nutrition – Shimla

Institute of Hotel Management, Catering & Applied Nutrition,

Kufri, Shimla was upgraded for Food Craft level to the Institute of Hotel Management level in the year 1996. It is located at Kufri on a land measuring 70 bighas. Second phase of the building of the Institute which is under construction will provide additional classrooms, conference rooms and auditorium. The girls hostel, guest suites and cafeteria are complete and are being handed over to the Institute shortly. The boys hostel is near completion stage and would be ready by 2004. The Institute offers 3-Year B.Sc. programme in Hospitality and Hotel Administration with an intake of 125 students. It also offers Craft Courses in Food & Beverage Service, Food Production and Post Graduate Diploma in Accommodation Operation & Management with an intake of 20, 60 and 30 students respectively.

Institute of Hotel Management, Catering Technology & Applied Nutrition – Srinagar

Institute of Hotel Management, Srinagar was established as the fifth Institute of Hotel Management in the year 1982. Moreover, the Institute has also started courses of very short duration for the local unorganized sector people associated with the Tourism & Hotels under the Central Government scheme of "Capacity Building for Service Providers" and the courses are being successfully conducted in the Institute as well as outside the Institute.

Institute of Hotel Management & Catering Technology – Thiruvananthapuram

Institute of Hotel Management and Catering Technology, Thiruvananthapuram, located in the capital city of Kerala, was established with a minimum annual intake of 120 students, a Post Graduate Diploma course in Accommodation Operation and Management (1½-Year) and also a Craft course in Food Production (1½-Year).

Indian Institute of Tourism and Travel Management (IITTM), Gwalior

Indian Institute of Tourism and Travel Management was established as a registered society in 1983 at New Delhi under the Ministry of Tourism with the objective of developing and promoting education, training and research in the field of travel and tourism. In August 1992, the Institute was shifted to Gwalior and is now functioning from its own campus spread over an area of 20 acres of land allotted by the State Government. In 1997, Eastern Regional Centre of IITTM was set up at Bhubaneswar from 2002-2003. The institute has started full-time Diploma in Tourism Management Programme (DTM). The Institute has been conducting full time Diploma in tourism Management (DTM) course at Gwalior since 1995-96 and at Bhubaneswar since 1996-97.

The Institute has also started 2-Year MBA programme from the academic session 2002-2004 at ITTTM, Gwalior. The Institute has been developing as a center of excellence for education and training in the field of tourism and travel management in the country.

IITTM offers academic opportunities to graduates and undergraduates directly and in collaboration with other reputed national and international institutes. The regular courses are offered to fresh graduates in pursuing their successful career in holiday and leisure management covering travel industries, tour operations, air cargo, interpretation etc. One-year full time AICTE approved DTM programme has been running successfully for the last 6-7 years at its main campus at Gwalior and Eastern Regional Centre at Bhubaneswar.

IITTM is designated as the International Focal Point (IFP) for Communication with links of the network of Asia-Pacific Education & Training Institute in Tourism (APETIT), which is promoted by United Nations Economic and Social Commission for Asia and the Pacific (UN-ESCAP), Bangkok, Thailand, with its objectives to strengthen the quantitative and qualitative resource for training, education and research in various countries in the Asia Pacific region, through collaboration and mutual cooperation.

Workshops/seminars on Inter Personal Communication, Personality Development and Interview Skills, Changing Scenario of Global Tourism were organized during 2001-2002 by IITTM.

Diploma in tourism and Travel Industry Management (DTTIM), a 16-month programme was restructured and modified into 9 month full-time/12 month part-time programme. The new restructured programme is presently being conducted at the Chapters of IITTM at New Delhi, Lucknow, Thiruvananthapuram, Ranchi, Guwahati and Ahmedabad. All the chapters are either State Government institutions or reputed Managemnt Institutions. To expand the network of IITTM, proposals from Uttaranchal, Karnataka and MP are under consideration.

SPM National Institute of Water Sports, Goa

The National Institute of Watersports has been set up on an 18-acre beach-side plot at Panaji, Goa in July 1990. Water-sports tourism is the ideal non-polluting industry for the under developed coastal regions of the country. As the only pioneering training establishment, NIWS has developed 20 different courses covering the entire range of water-sports. Since 1993, the Institute has conducted 280 courses for 5250 professionals from almost every state of the country.[9]

Conclusion

From the above discussion, it may be concluded that training is an act of increasing the knowledge and skill of an employee for doing a specified job. Development is future oriented training focusing on the personal growth of the employee. The basic objective of training is to help develop capacities and capabilities of employees and improve their level of performance. Orientation training is given to the new entrants for adapting himself to the new environment. In case of job training, the worker is trained on the job and at his work place. In apprenticeship training, the worker learns while observing his senior and helping him in the task. Refresher training helps in refreshing the memory of the employees. In vestibule training workers are trained in a training department by special instructors. A training centre is setup and actual job conditions are duplicated or stimulated in it. Training may range from highly specified instructions in the procedures to be adopted while performing a particular job, to very general instructions concerning economy and society. Selection of candidates for training should be made only after careful screening of the prospective employees for the effectiveness of the programme. A wide network for training and development of human resource for the tourism industry has been established in the country. Through planning based on 5 year plan, the government has made considerable investment on training of personnel in the tourism sector. The country has numerous institutes conducting courses from diploma and certificate level to post-graduate and research level in various fields related to tourism. The spectrum of training courses spans and covers numerous aspects of tourism for example, hotel management, hospitality, food craft and technology, accommodation management, food production, bakery and confectionary, catering and nutrition and so on. This wide network is bound to contribute tremendously to the growth and development of an Indian tourism sector. However, keeping in view the vast size of the country, the emerging requirements of the sector, the ever increasing number of foreign visitors to the country, growing emphasis of the states on their development of tourism potential and above all the foreign exchange contribution of the tourism sector, the current infrastructure for training and development of the human resource for tourism industry is far short of the demand. With a handful of training institutes sponsored and supported by the Government the tourism sector can not be fed fully for its human resource requirement. Hence there is need that private participation and investment must be made in this sector. The Government should encourage private sector to come forward for the establishment of training institutes which would go a long way for the growth of the sector.

The next chapter deals with a case study of Air Sahara, Jet Airways and ITDC.

REFERENCES

1. Flippo Edwin B. (1989), *Personnel Management*, McGraw Hill, Tokyo, p. 301.
2. Nadler Leonard (1984). *The Handbook of Human Resource Development (Glossary)*, John Wiley & Sons, New York, p. 136.

3 . Pascarella, Ernest T. and Terenzina, Patrick T. (1991). *How College Affects Students*. Jossey-Bass Publishers, San Francisco, p. 202.

4 . Tripathy, P.C. (2005). *Personnel Management and Industrial Relations*, Sultan Chand & Sons, New Delhi, p. 578.

5 . Kumar, Ramesh, (1992). *Training and Development Programmes for Managerial Effectiveness and Productivity, HRD for Productivity : Issues and Constraints*, Proceedings of 8th All India Management Congress, October 18-19, 1992, New Delhi, pp. 123-125.

6. Babu, Satish K.T. (1992). *Some Basic thoughts on Training and Management Development for Productivity', HRD : Productivity, issues and Constraints*, Proceedings of 8th All India Management Congress, Oct. 18-19, New Delhi, pp. 130-133.

7 . Punna Rao, P. and Reddy, M.S. (1992), *Human Resources Development Mechanisms for Extension Organizations*, Kalyani Publisher, New Delhi, p. 89.

8 . Annual Report (2003-04), Indian Tourism, Government of India, pp. 52-56.

9 . Annual Report, Ministry of Tourism, 2006-2007.

6

A Case Study of Air Sahara, Jet Airways and ITDC: Analysis and Interpretation

> "When a man wants to murder a tiger he calls it a sport; when the tiger wants to kill a man he call calls it ferocity."
>
> **—H.B. Shaw**

Full of all potential of all varied sorts, India is a significant and popular destination for tourist all over the world. It is a vast country which possesses a rich and varied heritage with diversity in its religions, culture and social outlook. As a result aviation has emerged as an important industry because of its linkage to the tourism sector. The aviation industry got a big leap when in the wake of liberalization, it has been opened to private sector. A number of private player, have entered into the aviation industry. The Indian government in its liberalization programme regularized operation by private airlines, thus acknowledging the Civil Aviation industry's importance in the promotion of tourism and as a result gain in foreign exchange earnings.

The private airline industry is healthy and now some of the private airlines have started flying on international routes too. The future out look for the industry augurs well. The business for the airlines industry in India is bound to grow faster.

Important amongst the private operators in aviation industry are AIR SAHARA and JET AIRWAYS. The Indian Tourism Development Corporation (ITDC) is the apex body which shoulders the responsibility for the overall development of the tourism sector. A case study of these organizations is presented in the following paragraphs:

AIR SAHARA

Air Sahara – One of India's Fastest growing Airlines. Air Sahara invites you to its world to feel and experience the touch of Sahara. For Air Sahara the vast expanse of the sky is its domain because it is through these spheres that it help reach these destinations day after day. Air Sahara strive to reach and attain heights in passenger care, comfort, reliability, safety and service.

The first flight, Air Sahara was born and gained freedom of the Indian skies with the launch of the open sky policy by the Government of India in 1990's. The first flight took off from Delhi to Mumbai on 3rd December, 1993 in a Boeing 737 aircraft.

At present, Air Sahara with 9th year of successful commercial operations has become India's premier domestic Airline. It covers 15 destinations with 67 flights offering more than 8250 seats per day with a current net strength of 11 latest generations Boeing aircraft. Air Sahara has placed tremendous importance on customer satisfaction (Appendix-II).

Sahara Airlines is one of the few domestic airlines in private sector, which has been able to survive successfully as a result of its customer oriented approach. The focus is one providing value added innovative services for passengers. Sahara Airlines is a pat of Sahara India Group which has major interests in Parabanking, Mass Communication, Housing & Infrastructure, International Trading, Domestic Marketing of Consumer Products and TV network.

The Group's current business level has touched USD 1700 million dollars with an asset base of approx. USD 2 billion. With the total work force of 6,00,000 and over 1342 offices all over the country, Sahara India Group is one of the most successful and diversified group in India. Sahara Airlines commenced operations from 3rd December 1993 as a scheduled airlines under new Aviation "Open Sky Policy" with 02 Boeing Aircraft

(Appendix-III). The airline had a simple aim, to provide international standard quality innovative service at excellent value for money for domestic travellers. From the early years of operation Sahara Airlines has grown to be the most innovative domestic airlines enjoying huge popularity and winning top global awards and international recognition. Sahara Airlines is now planning massive route expansion with hubs at Delhi and Mumbai. New value added products and services shall be introduced shortly with focus on the corporate travellers. In flight services, Ground services and city services are also being revamped.

In short, Sahara Airlines is all about customer care - A service offered in all the fleets, to all the passengers. At Sahara it is the firm belief to uphold the highest standards of traditional Indian hospitality, culture and courtesy. The highly trained personnel ensure that the trip is not only comfortable but a memorable one right from the time of check-in. The value additions such as flier services, Tele check-in, personalized Reading Kit and Meal Preference are at the highest standards in customer care and customer satisfaction.

Sahara Airline is interline partner of 53 international airlines. Some more agreements are in pipeline. British Airways, Air France, Lufthansa Airlines and SAS are amongst the list of interline partners of Sahara Airlines (Appendix IV).

To manage the business overseas and for the convenience of the passengers Sahara Airlines has established an office in London (Appendix-V).

Special Services of Sahara Airlines

Special services of the Airline can be broadly divided into:

(a) Ground Service

(b) In-flight Service

Ground Services

Sahara airlines believe in delivering the best to all its customers. It is this belief that is reflected in all its services. Flying Sahara

Airlines has a definite advantage because they believe in adding value to one's travel. Sahara Airlines offers its customers a variety of value added services that include:

Valet Service: To ensure sooth, swift and trouble free baggage handling exclusive valet service is provided at Sahara Airlines airport counters. In fact, there is no handling of baggage for the traveller. The Airlines courteous and dedicated valets will take all of your troubles and your baggage right out of your hands. While you shop, or buy a gift, or read at Sahara they believe that personalized services should give value of time and convenience to their passengers. Special care is taken to impart highest standard of training to the valets to make them efficient and effective in serving the esteemed customers. Air Sahara provide valet services at Delhi, Mumbai, Bangalore, Chennai and Lucknow.

Tele-Check in Service for Y/J: Sahara is the first domestic airline to offer Tele-check in facility for both economy and business class passengers. They now have dedicated lines on which one can access information on flights, timings, Frequent Flyer Programme and even ask for a seat of one's choice. All this is to ensure that you can access them at Sahara anytime, every time and at your convenience.

Fastest Baggage Retrieval: Baggage retrieval is the fastest among domestic airlines at Sahara. The baggage trolley reaches conveyor belt before the first passenger arrives at the arrival hall. They believe that the baggage should wait for the passenger but the passenger should not wait for his baggage.

Toll Free Numbers: 24 hours toll free numbers are installed at Delhi and Mumbai for easy access along with a customer call center to facilitate timely and accurate information to all passengers. They believe that a customer is never helpless with a Sahara toll free number with him.

Advance Seat Reservations: This facility is provided to both business and economy class passengers. The passenger can select and book his seat before he reaches the check in counter at the airport.

IVRS: Interactive Voice Responsive System is installed at Delhi and Mumbai airport. The passenger gets all the relevant flight information without spending the precious minutes holding the telephone lines. Soon the IVRS will be installed at Bangalore and Chennai as well.

Automated Flight Arrival/Departure Information: Sahara provides this facility 24 hours. The passengers can avail this facility and get the flight update immediately.

Lounge Facilities: This facility is provided to business class passengers. Sahara Airlines take immense pride in their tradition of care and service. The lounge gives the extra comfort and convenience.

City Check-in: Sahara believes in providing you with maximum comfort. Which is why they have introduced their new city check-in facility for passengers travelling with hard baggage. Now you don't have to arrive hours before take-off. Just drop in their City check in office at a convenient time one-day before departure and collect your boarding pass. The Sahara City Check in facility is currently available at Delhi, Mumbai, Bangalore, Chennai and Lucknow.

24 Reservation: Sahara airlines has 24 hours reservation offices at Mumbai, Delhi, Chennai.

Airport Transfers: Sahara offers free airport transfers from domestic to international airport vice-a-versa for interline passengers at Delhi and Mumbai.

Passengers with Restricted Mobility: Passengers with restricted mobility are given extra assistance. In case such a passenger is senior citizen customer service staff escorts him. If a passenger requires wheel chair he is provided with that facility as well.

Airport Lounges: At none of the airports they have Sahara airline's exclusive lounges but they have arrangements with airport restaurant where these facilities are there to earmark a separate portion for the Business class passengers.

Special features for Children and infants: Children and infants usually travel along with their parents and guardian. In case of unaccompanied children customer service staff render all assistance like checking in and escorting up to the aircraft and handing over to senior most cabin attendant on board the fight and on arrival such children are received by the commercial or customer service staff and handed over to the person nominated by the parents/guardian from the originating station. The parents of the infant have to pay for the return ticket of the deputed cabin attendant who finally hands over the infant to the nominated person at the destination.

Safety & Security

Air Sahara has its own X-ray machine and conducts periodic checks to assess the alertness of security system. Air Sahara also concentrates on air safety, and the cabin crew and in flight safety. The ground staff undergoes training in safety system.

Cancellation

If passengers cannot use their reservation, they should at once advice the airline concerned, well before departure of the flight, either through their travel agent or directly. In cancelling their reservation within the prescribed time limits, they are entitled to reimbursement for their ticket or to use it for another journey (except in case of some excursion fares). If passenger holding a confirmed reservation fail to present themselves for the flight concerned (no-show) the rest of their journey may be cancelled.

'No-show' and late cancellations cause the airlines loss of seating space and revenue. For this reason, certain penalties may be imposed on passengers when they claim reimbursement or make new reservations. Cancellation time limits may vary and therefore, individual airline's manuals should be consulted for verification.

Buy Tickets Online

- First domestic carrier in India to offer this option.
- User friendly and guided on-line booking process.

- Secure payment gateway through ICICI Bank Ltd.
- Instant confirmation given online.
- Book anytime from anywhere in the world.
- Log on the www.airsahara.net for bookings.

Fly today and Pay in Easy Instalments

- Adjoint promotion with standard chartered Bank.
- Exclusive benefits for standard chartered and associate credit card members.
- Available for both air tickets and exotic holidays.
- Balance amount debited as EMIs through monthly credit card statement in the next 8 months.

Introducing AIR Sahara Standard Chartered Cricket Credit Card

- Four-year validity for only Rs. 1500/- No annual fees.
- India's first Glo card.
- 15% off on Air Sahara tickets whenever India wins
- Global Acceptance – accepted by more than 19 million VISA establishments worldwide.
- Rewards Plus – earn points and redeem for air line tickets, luxury hotels, fashion accessories and much more.
- Instabuys – Use you Cricket card to fly Air Sahara and pay for your tickets/holidays in easy interest fee instalments.
- Credit period – enjoy 50 days of free credit.
- Global Emergency Assistance Service – while travelling overseas avail services for lost/stolen cards and get a instant card replacement.
- Free Personal Accident Insurance: Air Accident – 625000/-, Rail/Road 100000/-, Motorcycle & Pedestrian Accidents – 50000/-

Holiday Packages

These packages offer a wide range of hotels to suit the

individual budgets and time available. These holiday packages offer an excellent value for money as you get to fly in world class comforts as well as enjoy some of the finest hotels especially hand picked for your maximum comfort and flexibility. All this is conveniently designed for your as a single window convenience to shop for your travel, hotel stay, sight-seeing, food and local transportation requirements in one go. Our Domestic holiday package offering includes the following destinations – Goa, kerala, Karnataka, Sriangar, Hyderabad and Shridi.

Air Sahara Mobile SMS at 9844007272

- The convenience of short messaging service (SMS).
- On screen menu display of flight information.
- Extremely affordable with a maximum cost of Rs. 2 per message (depending upon network).
- Check in option available through SMS.
- Automatic flight status updates.
- One global number to access the Air Line.

Motive Behind Travel Agents Satisfaction Surveys

Satisfaction is a person's feelings of pleasure or disappointment resulting from comparing the service received in relation to the expectation. These expectation are formed by the past experiences, advertisements and the word of mouth and the best way to gauge the quality of the service is the customer's response. If the customers response is good or above average it is thought that company has succeeded in satisfying it's customers.

In the field of travel Air Sahara satisfies the customers through various travel agents. In real sense they are the Actual promoters of their field because they directly communicate with their customers.

The relationship and the expectation of the service industry by the middlemen to AIR SAHARA have been elaborated in the questionnaire as they are the ones who act as a bridge between the company and the customers. In the Aviation industry this important role is played by the travel agent. There are 26 authorized agents of AIR SAHARA in Lucknow.

All these agents are not only the authorized Agents of AIR Sahara but they also work on the behalf of all the major Airlines. That's why to know the customer's response regarding the services rendered to them by Air Sahara, first of all we have to survey the satisfaction level of our travel agents and for that purpose we designed a small questionnaire containing numerous questions regarding the performance of Air Sahara in comparison to its competitors.

The Travel Agents are considered to be important because they give a lot of business to the company.

Approximately 75% of the ticketing is done by the Agents and only 25% of the tickets are sold through the station office and Airport Counter.

JET AIRWAYS

Jet Airways is the biggest success story in the Indian aviation industry and one of the fastest growing airlines in the world.

They began operations with the mission of becoming the most preferred domestic airline in the country. Today, it's a matter of pride that they are widely recognized as "India's Best and world-class Domestic Airline".

On May 5, 1993, Jet Airways was set up with the objective of becoming the most preferred domestic airline in the country by providing high quality and reliable air travel in India. A very high percentage of the Indian domestic air traffic comprised business travellers. Therefore, their focus from the very beginning was to emerge as the "Businessman's Preferred Airline".

This led to a product and service design that aimed at world class norms in professional service and efficiency, beginning with the choice of aircraft itself.

Jet Airways operations began with a fleet of four Modern Generation Boeing 737-300 aircraft. The operation of these aircraft marked the first time they had flown Indian skies. They used the training facilities of Ansett (Australia) for the training and conversion of the pilots and engineers.

To help them achieve world class norms in service, Speedwing (a British Airways subsidiary), assisted them in conducting a programme on Customer Service Excellence for staff across functions at all levels.

To ensure accurate and efficient reservation systems Jet Airways tied up with and are co-hosted with SABRE – one of the world's best reservations systems. With three months of operation, they also became an associate member of IATA, a party to the IATA multilateral interline agreement and a member of the IATA clearing house.

Jet Airways achievements so far since their commencement, have been that they have achieved the status of the largest private domestic airline in India. The figures speak for themselves – from 4 aircraft in 1993-94 to 41 aircraft in February 2003; from 12 destinations in 1993-94 to 41 destinations in February 2003; from 24 daily flights in 1993-94 to over 250 flights in February 2003. In the process, they have carved out a market share of over 46% (estimated 2002-2003).

Their emphasis on technology and on time performance is one of the key factors of the spectacular success. They fly Modern and Next Generation aircraft and maintain a young aircraft fleet (with an average age of 3 years as on March 2003), making them one of the youngest fleet in the world.

Jet Airways operates over 250 flights daily to 42 destinations across the country. The rapid expansion of their route network has earned them the prestigious Air Transport World Award 2001 for Market Development and the "TTG Travel Award 2002" for Best Domestic Airline. Jet Airways were the first airline in India to receive the World Travel Market Global Award, the world's premier global travel event in London. They have also won the prestigious H&FS Domestic Airline of the Year Award four times, with the latest award in 2001. And Citibank Diners Club has chosen them as India's best domestic airline for the excellence in service besides consistently winning other awards for their excellence in service.

Jet Airways consists of the modern 737-400/700/800/900 and the ATR 72-500 and on having an unbeatable record of on-time flights and providing world-class frequent flyer benefits to their customers, through their alliances with British Airways, KLM Royal Dutch Airlines and Northwest Airlines. They strive to provide service of the highest standard to their customers, both on ground and in-flight. Jet Airways is proud that they are one of the few airlines in the world to receive the ISO 9001 certification for their in-flight services (Appendix-VI).

Apart from the various innovations launched by them in the history of Indian aviation, Jet Airways also continue to be a responsible corporate citizen.

In jet airways the main stress is given to the service and the words of mouth are the main source of publicity. Jet Airways keeps up its motto that is 'the Joy of Flying'. The logo, which is at the tail of Jet Airways, symbolizes rising sun, which represents strong dedication and care for its people (Appendix-VII).

Services offered by the Jet Airways on the Ground

Jet Airways provide entire range of facilities designed for the convenience of passengers, from reservation and check-in, to in-flight services, speedy baggage recovery and more to make the flight on Jet Airways a comfortable, safe and memorable experience.

Ticket Counters

Jet Airways ticket counters are conveniently located at all the destinations within its network, both in the city and at the airport. They now also have a computerized ticketing facility at most stations.

Airport Check in Time

Check in time is one and a half hours prior to departure. Most stations have tele-check-in facilities for club premiere passengers travelling with only hand baggage. They may tele check-in 3 hours to 45 minutes prior to departure and must arrive at the airport check-in-counter 30 minutes prior to departures.

Seat Request

Club Premiere passengers can book their choice of seat at the time of reservation.

Meal Request

All jet Airways passengers are requested to indicate their meal preferences at the time of reservation (Appendix-VIII).

24-Hour Reservations

In Mumbai, Delhi and Bangalore, Jet Airways offers passengers a 24-hour reservation service. It is being extended in other big cities also which come under Jet Airways network.

Airport Lounges

Club Premiere passengers can avail lounge facilities at certain airports. Passengers are offered complimentary beverages and snacks in these lounges.

Value Added Services (Jet Privilege)

Jet privilege is the Frequent flier programme of Jet Airways. The jet privilege programme offers members an unmatched mix of rewards and privileges. In addition to the exclusive facilities Jet privilege members can now exchange their miles for free flights on the British Airways worldwide network, spanning 174 destinations across the world. Jet privilege members can also exchange their miles on the KLM Global network, covering more than 81 countries across six continents or on the Northwest network covering more than 400 cities in the world.

International through Check in Facility

As a customer of Jet Airways, one can avail of the facility of through check-in if one has a connecting flight into or out of the country. This means at the first check in point, passengers' luggage will be checked in, pre labeled and boarding passes/ baggage tags issued up to their final destinations. They also provide this facility from one destination to other within India.

City Check-in

Jet Airways has introduced check-in counters at their reservations offices in the Metropolitan cities. This facility allows passengers with only hand baggage to check-in and collect their boarding pass at the city office at least 2 hours before the flight time. Passengers availing this facility have to report at the boarding gate 15 minutes before the departure.

Caring for the Disabled

Handicapped and infirm passengers can make a request while booking their flight and an attendant with wheelchair will be arranged.

Baggage Clearance

Jet Airways ensures speedy baggage clearance and delivery on arrival at all destinations.

Coach Service

Jet Airways operates a complimentary airconditioned luxury shuttle coach service between Mumbai's Sahar and Santacruz airport for passengers connecting between international and domestic flights (Appendix-IX).

Interline Transfers

Jet Airways has interline agreement with over 120 international airlines which allows convenient transfer of passengers from one carrier to another.

Services offered by the Jet Airways in the Sky Comfort

In Jet Airways club premiere seats are fitted with arm-rest tables, and arranged in a two by two configuration so that every passenger has a window or aisle seat. The seat pitch is luxurious 38 inches. Even in the economy class it is spacious 31 inches.

Infant and Child Care

Jetkids is the special programme for children between 2-12 which provides exciting gifts to make the flying experience of the younger patrons more enjoyable. Also they provides assistance if one require to change the nappies of the infants.

Sleep Easy

Pillows and blankets are available on request on all the routes.

Reading Material

Every Jet Airways flight has a wide range of news paper and magazines.

Towels

Jet Airways passengers on most routes are welcomed abroad with refreshing hot and cold towels.

Food and Beverage

Jet Airways provides wide range of food and beverage on the flight. They rotate the meals every day for four day and change the entire menu every six months.

Beef and pork are not served, meet products served are halal. All food is cooked in pure vegetable oil. Special meals-dibetic, low cholesterol, medical, jain and baby meals are also available. However it must be asked 24 hours prior to departure.

First Aid

Like other airlines First Aid kit is also available with the cabin crew.

Safety

Safety instructions and emergency procedures are explained by the cabin crew on each flight the seat belt must be fastened at take off and landing and when ever the seat belt sign is on, the seat back rest must be in an upright position and trey table must be stowed away at take off and landing.

Smoking

The government of India prohibits smoking on all domestic flights. As a separate precautionary measures, all toilets in the plane are fitted with smoke detectors.

Electronic Devices

The Government of India prohibits the use of mobile phones, CD players and pagers, as these interfere with aircraft communications and radio navigation systems.

Landing

Flight deck crew will generally try and give the smoothest landing possible. However, at times, safety considerations require that firmer landings be performed. Conditions that may require this include: shorter runways, wind blowing across the runway or turbulent conditions, water ponds forming on the runway in heavy rains.

Jet Airways Presents Jet Elite for Its Privilege Customer

Customers who are flying by the JET Airways have a wider choice of cities, hotels and better discounts to choose under its scheme JET ELITE, as a business traveller one have hectic schedules with little time for relaxations. Keeping in mind JET Airways have attractive discounts to offer at some of the best hotels in the country (Appendix-X).

A Study of Merger of Air Sahara and Jet Airways

Domestic airline Air Sahara seems to have hit some financial turbulence. When contacted, Air Sahara CEO told that the poor performance was due to under utilization of its fleet, mainly because of the non-availability of pilots.

He expects that the performance will improve in the second half of the year, the main business season for the airlines. There are plans afoot to lease three new aircraft by January 2006. Backed by new aircraft and additional domestic and international routes, the E&Y report projects a revenue increase of 98% for the next financial year.

Meanwhile, the rescue plan appears to have run into a wall, at least with domestic suitors. In end, July, before E&Y came into the picture, Spice Jet had almost signed on the dotted line with Air Sahara to acquire a substantial stake. But just before the deal could be inked, E&Y is said to have persuaded Air

Sahara to set new terms and conditions that help protect its interests. The domestic suitors, who were perhaps hoping for easy pickings, now find the new valuations too bitter to swallow.

"We were close to signing the deal until Ernst & Young jumped into the fray and promised the moon to Air Sahara. The valuation of the company, as suggested by E&Y, is irritational and is based on hypothetical profitability projections. We are clearly not interested in pouring hundreds of crores into a business where we do not get any management control", a source close to Spice Jet said. A source close to Kingfisher Airines said, "we are clearly not interested in the deal with its current price tag. We have offered a price beyond which the deal makes no business sense. The valuation suggested by the company far exceeds the company's worth in terms of its assets and profitability".

E&Y, on the other hand, is understood to have now approached potential international investors. For domestic airlines in India, despite its current shortcomings, Air Sahara remains an attractive target. The real ace up its sleeve is its flying rights to lucrative overseas destinations. The new domestic carriers, as per current regulations, require five years' operating experience within India before they are allowed to fly abroad.[1]

It has seen the pomp and the grandeur of their weddings. It has seen them sponsor the Indian cricket team and also build exclusive Swiss style villas for celebrities like Aishwarya Rai and Sachin Tendulkar. But there's one thing about the Sahara Parivar that has always been shrouded in secrecy – the status of their financial health.

Pilots Jittery as Jet Snaps Up Air Sahara

The Jet Airways on 20 Jan. 2006 tightened its grip at the top of India's domestic airline industry, agreeing to purchase its smaller rival Air Sahara for $500 million in an all-cash deal. Under the agreement between the two carriers, sources said, a unified entity is expected to start flight in the Indian skies with the beginning of the 2006-07 fiscal.

Though Sahara India Pariwar chief assured that all jobs will be protected, around 12 of its bombardier CRJ pilots have put in their papers since both airlines announced two weeks back that a deal is in the offing. Though Air Sahara executive denied the move, a pilot source said: "We feel it's better to look at options outside rather than join the merged airline where we are not sure if Jet will use the Bombardier fleet for long".

The sources revealed that the Air Sahara staff would be absorbed only on 'merit basis'. Officials close to the deal pointed out that efforts are already underway to ensure a smooth merger of assets. "An integration team has been set up to merge the two entities, its systems and operations.

Regulatory approvals for the deal are now being sought and if all clearances are in place, the unified airline will be in operations from April 2006.

Under the deal, Jet will acquire only the assets of Air Sahara, which will include the latter's leased fleet of 27 aircraft, ground handling equipment, parking slots, inventories and aircraft spares. Jet Airways are not planning to make it (Sahara) a low-cost carrier".

Though Jet Airways will, in the interim period, continue to use the Air Sahara brand, the same would be phased out gradually and all Sahara planes would be don the Jet livery.[2]

The officials sought to allay the fears about the deal, saying: "There's no problem about the Lal. I have got information that we have received the approval from the Department of Company Affairs. We are completing necessary formalities of the acquisition". Sahara, too, scotched all talks of the deal running into trouble.

The two companies had signed an agreement and opened an escrow account, which is set to expire on March 24. Jet Airways are awaiting the regulatory approvals. Sahara officials also said the finer modalities of the deal were being thrashed out.

The sudden delay comes within days of Jet Airways stating

that it is yet to seek government approval for the deal. The deal – announced on January 19 – was touted as the largest acquisition in the Indian skies to create a single airline that would control nearly 48% of the market.

The director-general (investigations and registrations) – the investigating arm of Monopolies and Restrictive Trade Practices Commission (MRTPC) – issued notices to both the air carriers about details of the proposed acquisition. DGIR is looking into the mega deal to check whether it has resulted in creating a monopoly in the Indian aviation sector.

Asked whether the DGIR could also approach the Registrar of Companies to seek details of the board meetings regarding the sale and purchase process, the sources said it could be a possibility. "All these aspects are being looked into", a source said, The MRTPC, which swung into action after PMO intervened, had forwarded the investigation of the deal to the DGIR in the wake of reports as well as accusations that it could lead to monopoly of Jet Airways.[3]

The takeover of Air Sahara by Jet Airways for Rs. 2,300 crore early this year has come under the scrutiny of Monopolies and Restrictive Trade Practices Commission, which is likely to issue a notice to the buyer.

Since the deal helped Jet increase its share in the domestic market to over 50%, the Commission is looking into the monopoly aspect following a complaint.

Sources in the Commission said that a notice could be issued to Jet. Jet officials, however, were not aware of the development saying that they had not heard anything from the Commission. The Jet executive director said: 'We have not got any communication from the MRTPC. Anyway, where is the question of monopoly when already five other airlines are operating in the country".

Immediately after the deal, MRTPC chairperson said the deal did not appear to warrant any immediate probe.[4]

There have been rumours of cash strain, but no real data

has emerged. Now, documents available with TOI suggest that Air Sahara, the group's airline, is in a degree of financial strife. The airline has an accumulated loss of Rs. 100 crore and is likely to end the year with Rs. 118 crore of losses on its books. It is expected to report net loss of Rs. 17 crore for this fiscal, against a profit of Rs. 32 crore last year.[5]

India's largest private airline Jet Airways $560 million (Rs. 2,4520 crore) bid to acquire its smaller rival Air Sahara has hit a slight stumbling block with both the carriers unable to land on a common ground over branding matters. Sources close to the negotiations pointed out that the top honchos of both Jet and Sahara – who met in Lucknow on 11.1.06 could not conclude the deal as issues regarding the future of Air Sahara brand could not be settled.

The final agreement, sources said, is expected to be finalized by January 15 – when Jet's broad is slated to take up the matter. "While the Sahara India Pariwar wants the Air Sahara brand to continue even after it exits the venture, Jet is keen on using only its own brand for the combined entity", a source told "the Times of India. "The discussions were held on 11.1.06, but they were inconclusive as the branding issues are yet to be sorted out, "the source added.

As per the ongoing negotiations, jet has offered to acquire the entire airline operations of Air Sahara – including its aircraft assets and debt liabilities. However, Air Sahara officials termed it a strategic alliance aimed at consolidating their strengths and growing together.

"We realize that it's time now for consolidation in the Indian airline industry. So, we are talking to Jet Airways for a strategic relationship to work towards a better tomorrow. As we move forward with the talks, the contours of this relationship will be finalized. All I can say now is that the talks are for a strategic relationship, and there are no timelines for finalizing the agreement", Air Sahara executive vice president said.

Jet Airways spokesperson also confirmed that negotiations are underway for an alliance, but refused to divulge details.

"Our officials and investment advisors are studying the matter. We are in negotiations with Air Sahara but a final deal has not been inked yet".

The deal would give Jet, which already controls about 40% of the domestic market, a share of over 50%, putting it way beyond India Airlines' 30% or so. This, some analysts said, could prove to be the only stumbling bloc on its path as it would give Jet Airways a monopoly in the domestic airline market and be against the spirit of the competition policy.

Two other domestic airline players – Kingfisher Airlines and Spicejet – were also in the race for Air Sahara, but have now opted out in view of the high valuation sought by its management.

Air Sahara had stated that Ernst and Young have valued the airline between $750 million and $1 billion. While Kingfisher had offered $600 million for acquiring Air Sahara – which included $200 million as cash – SpiceJet had sought to split the airline's domestic and international operations and buy just the local operations for around $200 million.

It may be concluded that –

- Sahara wants its brand to be retained even after sell-off, but Jet wants to use its own brand.
- Jet has offered to buy the entire operations of Air Sahara, including aircraft assets and debt liabilities, for $560m.
- It would give Jet control of 40% of the domestic market, a share of over 50%.[6]

India's biggest aviation deal between jet Airways and Air Sahara seems to be heading for rough weather. Delays in getting a clear government view on key issues – particularly those relating to transfer of Sahara's landing and parking rights across the country – is threatening to delay a final agreement between the two private airlines (Appendix-XI).

Though Jet Airways chairman scotched speculation that the deal was in trouble, sources claimed that a lack of clarity on the issue of transferring Sahara's rights might force a renegotiation on the timing of the deal.

Removing a major obstacle in the way of Jet Airways' takeover of Air Sahara, a high level official committee on 20.5.06 cleared 100% transfer of all assets of one company to the other.

The Aircraft Acquisition Committee, including offices of the civil aviation ministry, Directorate General of Civil Aviation (DGCA) and Airports Authority of India, has cleared the transfer of properties, including issues relating to parking bays and slots. However, these rights cannot be further transferred or lease to a third party.

The Committee has finalized its guidelines on merger and acquisitions and would be sending them to the civil aviation ministry very soon for its approval.

The guidelines would enable the proposed merger of two state-owned carriers Air India and Indian Airlines. Such a merger would enable the national carriers to not only face domestic competition from Jet Sahara deal, but also on the international front, especially from large airlines like Singapore Airlines, British Airways, Malaysian Airlines and Emirates.[7]

INDIA TOURISM DEVELOPMENT CORPORATION (ITDC)

India Tourism Development Corporation was established in 1966 as an autonomous public sector corporation. ITDC was entrusted with the task of helping in the development of tourism infrastructure and promote India as a tourist destination. Today, ITDC provides a complete package of tourism services including accommodation, catering, transport, publicity and hotel consultancy, duty free shops, an in house travel agency, entertainment and shopping.

ITDC's Accommodation Chain

The Ashok Group – is the largest in the country. It offers accommodation ranging from luxury suites to modestly furnished rooms, from beach resorts to a moderately priced forest lodge. Almost 4000 rooms are scattered throughout India.

The Government of India in 1965 established Department of Tourism in the three separate corporations, viz. Hotel Corporation of India Ltd., India Tourism Corporation Ltd. and India Tourism Transport Undertaking Ltd. These corporations were setup under the provision of Companies Act, 1956. The main functions of these corporations were to construct and manage hotels in the public sector, produce material for tourist publicity and to provide transport facilities to the tourists.

Board of Directors

ITDC is a Public Sector Enterprise and the appointment of Directors both executive and non-executive is made by the Government of India. The reconstitution of the ITDC Board of Directors with appointment of non-official part-time Directors remained under consideration of the Ministry during the year 2003-04. The Board has now been reconstituted with effect from 1.10.2004 by induction of two part-time Government Directors. Presently, the Board of Directors comprises of Chairman & Managing Director and three part-time official Directors representing Government of India.

Organisational Set-up

The Organisational set up at the corporate level comprises three business groups viz., Hotels and catering, Duty Free Trade and Ashok Travels 7 Tours. Besides, there are some support services department namely personnel, F&A, Hotel sales, HRP and Training, MMD, Project Engineering, P&P and Vigilance & Security. In addition, there are four Regional offices at Delhi, Mumbai, Chennai and Kolkata (Appendix-XII).

Human Resource Management

With a view to rationalizing Human Resource, VRS was introduced and 274 employees have opted for the same. The total number of employees in the Corporation decreased from 3498 as on 31st March, 2003 to 3125 as on 31st March, 2004. Of these, 903 employees belong to Scheduled Castes (SC), 66 employees belong to Scheduled Tribes (ST), and 95 employees to Other Backward Classes (OBC). No recruitment took place during the year 2003-04. 20 employees were promoted during the year, out of whom 2 belong to SC and one to OBC. Further, there are 367 women employees working in ITDC as on 31st March 2004 constituting 11.74% of the total workforce of the Corporation. Of these, 52 are at executive level and 315 at non-executive level.

India's Hotel for the World – Ashok Group of Hotels

The Ashok Group of Hotels now comprises of eight owned hotels viz. Ashok Hotel, Hotel Samrat and Hotel Janpath at New Delhi and Hotels at Mysore, Bhubaneswar, Patna, Jammu & Jaipur and six point venture Hotels, 3 DoT properties and one Airport Restaurant at IGI Airport, New Delhi managed by ITDC. During the year under review, the overall occupancy of Ashok Group of Hotels increased from 44% to 47%. The turnover of hotels has also increased to Rs. 100.77 crores in 2003-04 from Rs. 91.48 crores in 2002-03.

ITDC is operating six joint venture hotels at Ranchi, Guwahati, Itanagar, Pondicherry, Bhopal and Puri. As a result of aggressive corporate monitoring, some of the joint ventures have started showing profits (Appendix-XIII).

Duty Free Shops

The ITDC operates 37 Duty Free Shops at international airports in Delhi, Mumbai, Chennai, Calcutta, Thiruvananthapuram and Goa and one down town duty free shop at Ashok Hotel, New Delhi. During the year 2003-04, special discounts were offered and periodical sales promotions were carried out to attract visitors. But in the year 2004-05 its financial position has improved.

Duty Free Shops – Their Turnover and Profits

To facilitate shopping for international travellers, ITDC operates a network of 37 user-friendly Duty Free Shops in all the International Airports in the country. Its Duty Free Shops at Delhi, Mumbai, Calcutta, Chennai, Thiruvananthapuram and Goa offer the best bargains in quality merchandise, quick customer friendly service and the widest choice of over 25,000 international and Indian brands: from world-class brands of wines, liquor, cigarettes, writing instruments, perfumes to authentic Indian handicrafts and handlooms, gift items, the finest Indian tea, silk carpets, intricate wood carvings and much more.

Apart from providing duty free shopping at departure and arrival lounges of international airports, ITDC has extended the Duty Free Shopping privilege through Down Town Duty Free Shopping. The first of such Duty Free Shops has been opened at The Ashok Hotel, New Delhi. One has to just check-in at the Down Town Duty Free Shop with valid passport and international flight ticket and has the leisure of duty free shopping. The merchandise is delivered at the departure hall of the international airport.

ITDC has also planned to set up five new shops at the upcoming new International Airports of Bangalore, Ahmedabad, Hyderabad, Varanasi and Calicut. Plans are also afoot to open Duty paid shops in metropolitan cities which have potential for marketing of international and upmarket merchandise.

In 1995-96 Duty Free Shops accounted for about 38 per cent of ITDC's profits. The turnover in 1996-97 increased from Rs. 74.11 crores to Rs. 77.70 crores reflecting an increase of 4.8 per cent and the net profit increased from Rs. 28.68 crores showing an increase of 5.2 per cent over the previous year.

In the year 1997-98 the figure was 54 per cent which means that ITDC garners more money from Duty Free Shops than the 26 hotels it runs. The Corporation made a net profit of just Rs. 25 crores from the hotels in 1997-98 while those from Duty Free Shops were Rs. 29 crore. The Duty Free Trade division increased its turnover marginally from Rs. 83.53 crores to Rs. 84.04 crores during 1998-99 despite economic crisis in the Asian Pacific Region where most Duty Free Shops showed a downward trend. Sale of goods from duty free shops was of the order of Rs. 90.83 crores in 2003 and Rs. 110.28 crores in 2004.

The tourism scenario during 1998-99 has not been encouraging and conducive mainly due to general recession in

Table 6.1

Financial Performance of India Tourism Development Corporation

Particulars	*Amount (Rs. In crores)*								
	1998-99	*1999-00*	*2000-01*	*2001-02*	*2002-03*	*2003-04*	*2004-05*	*2005-06*	*2006-07*
Sales Turnover	297.10	288.50	305.60	184.44	238.40	290.65	363.49	373.64	362.65
Operating Profit (Before Interest & Depreciation)	18.48	(-)17.05	(-)22.81	(-)32.34	2.79	7.52	37.94	54.53	48.92
Profit Before Tax	12.02	(-)24.03	(-)33.62	(-)36.55	(-)1.21	2.75	31.16	51.57	45.65
Profit After Tax	10.81	(-)24.04	(-)33.63	(-)32.86	1.19	2.75	28.77	45.79	45.65
Foreign Exchange	107.36	107.77	105.87	79.00	100.77	113.57	156.59	146.93	104.37

Source: Annual Report, (2006-07) India Tourism, Government of India, p. 116.

the economy, drop in business and corporate traffic, economic shake-up of Far east countries making them economical for the foreign tourists, increase in operating costs, etc. The performance of hospitality industry was, therefore, adversely affected in private as well as public sector.

It is noted from Table 6.1 that the turnover during 1998-99 decreased by 5.1% to Rs. 297.10 crores compared to Rs. 313.20 crores in 1997-98, operating profit declined to 69.7% from Rs. 60.97 crores in 1997-98 to Rs. 18.48 crores and the net profit decreased by 75% from Rs. 43.30 crores in 1997-98 to Rs. 10.81 crores.

With the improvement in tourism scenario, the performance of ITDC improved during 2003-2004. The turnover of the Corporation increased to 290.65 crores during 2003-2004 from Rs. 238.40 crores in 2002-2003, representing an increase of 22.4%. The operating profit also increased from Rs. 2.79 crores in 2002-2003 to Rs. 7.52 crores during 2003-2004.

The year 2005-06 shown improvement in financial performance of ITDC. The turnover of the corporation increased from Rs. 636.49 crore in 2004-05 to Rs. 373.64 crore in 2005-06. The profit (before tax) increased substantially from Rs. 31.16 crore in 2004-05 to Rs. 51.57 crore in 2005-06.

During the year 2006-07 (up to December 2006) the financial performance further improved as compare to the corresponding period last year. The turnover during 2006-07 (upto December 2006) was Rs. 362.65 crores (provisional) as compared to Rs. 265.92 crore during the corresponding period last year. During this period the operating profit of Rs. 18.24 crore during the corresponding period last year.

Disinvestments in ITDC

ITDC was one of the first PSUs to be referred to the Disinvestment Commission. In its report submitted to the Government in February 1997, the Commission recommended that the prime properties be given to leading hotel chains through a competitive bidding process to run on a long term contract basis. The other hotels should be demerged and all its shares sold to interested parties on a competitive basis. The report said that the Governments had no role to play in the hotel business and it should get out, once the workers interest were taken care off.

In January, 2000, the Disinvestment Commission took the decision to hawk 31 of 33 ITDC hotels to the right buyers. Their appalling performance has lent a sense of urgency to the government decision to put them on the chopping block.

Disinvestment of ITDC hotels is still on and five hotel properties viz. (i) Hotel Jaipur Ashok, Jaipur (ii) Hotel Kalinga Ashok, Bhubaneswar, (iii) Hotel Pataliputra Ashok, Patna, (iv) Hotel Jammu Ashok, Jammu and (v) Hotel Janpath, New Delhi are currently in the process of being disinvested. Action has also been initiated by the Ministry of Disinvestment for disinvestments of joint venture hotel properties of ITDC.

Test of Hypotheses

The hypotheses of this study have been tested with the use of appropriate statistical tools such as mean, standard deviation, skewness and chi-square. Finally, the findings of the study and summary of conclusions have been given. Based on these findings, suggestions and recommendations have been made for the human resource planning in globalizing Indian tourism industry to face the challenges of 21st century.

Ho_1 Unplanned Human Resource planning leads to poor productivity in tourism sector in India.

Ho_2 Any expenditure exercise made in planning and development of tourism Human Resource increases the cost of Human Resource and adds less to profitability in tourism sector.

Ho_3 Poor Human Resource Planning leads to unencouraging profitability in tourism sector in India.

Ho_4 In most of the tourism organizations human resource information system has not been fully developed and thus it is not possible to develop effective human resource plans.

Analysis and Interpretation

It is evident from Table 6.2 that majority of the employees agree with the statements of regular assessment of the surplus and shortage of human resources of ITDC for present and future requirements. The mean value is slightly higher than the average standard score i.e. 3 at five point scale. The variation in the opinion is 1.1605, while skewness is -0.016. It shows that opinion is distributed more towards higher side of the average score. The calculated value of the c^2 is significant at 1 percent level of significance. It indicates that opinion of the respondents is not equally distributed. Thus the above analysis leads to the conclusion that most of the respondents agree with the opinion that top management needs to impart knowledge and develop skills oriented to the nature and needs of the ITDC for present and future requirements.

As far as determination of levels of future recruitment and selection needs are concerned, the majority of the responses do not agree with the same. The mean value of the responses depicts that majority of the responses are lying towards lower side of the mean standard score at five point scale. The standard Deviation and skewness are noted 1.1955 and .475 respectively. Further c^2 value is significant at 1 percent level of significance. It shows that opinion of the respondents is not equally distributed. Thus, it can be concluded that they are not satisfied with the efforts to identify and utilize the potential of the employees.

Table further shows that majority of the respondents are uncertain about their opinion regarding determination of future training and management development needs. The mean value of the responses is slightly lower than the average standard score at five point scale. The standard deviation and skewness are noted 1.1197 and .082 respectively. It shows that majority of the responses are distributed more towards higher side of the mean score. The c^2 value is significant at 1percent level of significance. Thus the opinion of the respondents is not equally distributed. It leads to the conclusion that majority of the respondents do not have the same opinion over the issue of present selection procedure adopted by ITDC.

It is notable that majority of the respondents, are uncertain over the issue of controlling of wage and salary costs. The value of the mean score is less than the average standard score, which shows that opinions of the respondents is distributed more towards lower side The standard deviation and skewness are 1.0057 and .053 respectively. The calculated value of c^2 is higher than the table value and thus it rejects Ho at 1 percent level of significance. It leads to the conclusion that majority respondents are not satisfied over the issue to enrich the individual intellectually as well as materially to enable him/her lead happier life by developing his/her capacity to learn and earn.

Table 6.2 exhibits that majority respondents are uncertain over the issue of optimum utilization of human resource employed through HRP keeping in view the requirements in ITDC. The mean score of the respondents is slightly more than the average standard score. The variation in the opinion and skewness are noted 1.1811 and .014 respectively. The c^2 value is significant at 1 percent level of significance. It leads to the conclusion that opinion of the respondents is not equally distributed over this issue. Further, it may be concluded that majority of the respondents do not agree with the provisions related to properly planned, developed and monitored the HRP system considering the ITDC requirements.

Further, it is noted from Table 6.2 that majority of the respondents are uncertain regarding provision of a basis for future management development programmes. The mean score is slightly less than the average standard score at five point scale. The calculated value of c^2 is significant at one percent level of significance. This shows that responses of the employees are not equally distributed over the issue of recognition of the importance of different type of financial benefits in ITDC. It is distributed more towards lower side of the average standard score, which supports the opinion that they are not satisfied with the recognition of these benefits.

Employees' attitude to make efforts to meet the needs of expansion and diversification programmes has been analysed on the basis of the opinion of the respondents. It is observed

TABLE 6.2

India Tourism Development Corporation

Management/Employees Attitude and Human Resource Planning

Name of Responses	Scaling	Number of Factors											
		To assess regu-larlythe surplus and shortage of human resources		Determination of levels of future recruitment and selection needs		Determination of future training and management develo pment needs		Controlling of wage and salary costs		To ensure opti-mum utilization of human re sources employed		To provide a basis for future manage mentdevelopment programmes	
		Frequency	%age	Frequency	%age	Frequency	%age	Frequency	%age	Frequency	%age	Frequency	%age
Strongly agree	5	12	9.6	9	7.2	7	5.6	5	4.0	16	12.8	13	10.4
Agree	4	36	28.8	18	14.4	29	23.2	30	24.0	24	19.2	26	20.8
Disagree	2	35	28.0	41	32.8	26	20.8	38	30.4	25	20.0	34	27.2
Strongly Disagree	1	12	9.6	28	22.4	19	15.2	10	8.0	15	12.0	15	12.0
Uncertain	3	30	24.0	29	23.2	44	35.2	42	33.6	45	36.0	37	29.6
Total		125	100	125	100	125	100	125	100	125	100	125	100.0
Mean		3.0080		2.5120		2.8320		2.8560		3.0080		2.9040	
S.D.		1.1605		1.1955		1.1197		1.0057		1.1811		1.1738	
Skewness		-.016		.475		.082		.053		.014		.128	
Standard Error of Skewness		.217		.217		.217		.217		.217		.217	
χ^2		23.360		23.440		29.520		44.320		41.840		23.560	
P		0.01		<0.01		<0.01		<0.01		<0.01		<0.01	

Strongly agree	5	5	4.0	4	3.2	7	5.6	4	3.2	9	7.2	6	4.8
Agree	4	21	16.8	19	15.2	29	23.2	25	20.0	23	18.4	13	10.4
Disagree	2	42	33.6	46	36.8	35	28.0	32	25.6	41	32.8	46	36.8
Strongly Disagree	1	16	12.8	36	28.8	20	16.0	12	9.6	12	9.6	35	28.0
Uncertain	3	41	32.8	20	16.0	34	27.2	52	41.6	40	32.0	25	20.0
Total		125	100	125	100	125	100	125	100	125	100	125	100
Mean		2.6560		2.2720		2.7440		2.8160		2.8080		2.2720	
S.D.		1.0326		1.1315		1.1494		.9704		1.0754		1.1243	
Skewness		.242		.633		.097		-.052		.273		.724	
Standard Error of Skewness		.217		.217		.217		.217		.217		.217	
χ^2		41.680		42.560		21.840		55.520		36.400		41.840	
P		<0.01		<0.01		<0.01		<0.01		<0.01		<0.01	

Source: Data collected through questionnaire.

that their opinion is distributed more towards lower side i.e. uncertain to disagree. The mean value is noted lower than the average standard score, while variation in the opinion and skewness is noted 1.0326 and .242 respectively. This supports the above analysis. Further c^2 test is significant at one percent level of significance. It reveals that opinion of the respondents are not equally distributed. Thus above analysis, leads to the conclusion that ITDC is lacking in lying emphasis on the development of managerial capabilities.

Table 6.2 depicts that majority of the respondents either disagree or strongly disagree with the provision of full development of human resource information system in ITDC. The mean value, standard deviation and skewness indicate that their opinion is distributed towards lower side on the issue. The calculated value of c^2 shows the significant results at 1 percent level of significance. The conclusion can be drawn that majority of the respondents disagree with the update of the knowledge and skills of management through career counselling and short duration programmes in ITDC.

As far as respondent attitude towards slow growth of productivity in ITDC is concerned they do agree with the statement. The mean value, standard deviation and skewness support the above opinion. The significant value of c^2 depicts that there is significant variation in the opinion of respondents over the issue. The above analysis leads to the conclusion that their opinions are distributed towards lower side. It further concludes that employees do agree with the slow growth of productivity of ITDC.

The Table 6.2 reveals that majority of the responses are distributed more towards lower side over the issue of unplanned Human Resource planning which leads to poor productivity. The mean value support the above opinion. The variation in the opinion and skewness are observed .9704 and –.052 respectively. The calculated value of c^2 shows significant results at one percent level of significance. It is concluded that Appraisal Factors are still to be added more.

The majority of the respondents do not agree with the poor Human Resource Planning which leads to unencouraging profitability in ITDC. The mean value is found lower side of the average standard score i.e. 3 at 5 point scale. This shows that their opinion is distributed more towards uncertain to disagree side. The standard deviation and skewness also supports the above opinion. While calculating the c^2 value, it is significant at one percent level of significance. It shows that opinion of the respondents is not equally distributed. Thus, it can be concluded that any expenditure made in planning and development of Human Resource increases the cost of Human Resource and adds less to profitability concerned, the majority of the employees are not satisfied.

Thus, the above analysis leads to overall conclusion that majority of the respondents are not satisfied with the various statements given for ITDC.

In order to make case studies of Air Sahara and Jet Airways, the questionnaire is designed to find out the opinions of the employees (now below the rank of Asstt. Managers and Supervisory level) regarding the Human Resource Planning in tourism sector in India. The questionnaire consists of 28 statements which are related to forecasting future requirements for human resources, determination of future recruitment and selection needs, linking human resource planning with organsiational planning, providing a basis for future management development programmes, ensuring optimum utilization of human resources presently employed, assessing the surplus and shortage of human resources, control of wage and salary costs, facilitating productivity bargaining and so on. For primary survey, a sample of 100 employees have been selected for the study to find out their opinions related to Human Resource Planning. The purpose of the present questionnaire is to serve the objective of human resource planning which is to maintain and improve the organisation's ability to achieve its goal by developing strategies that will result in optimum contribution of human resources and thereby help to improve productivity at dynamic levels of adequacy.

TABLE 6.3

AIR SASHARA

Chi-square Value

Agreed statements (A)		*Disagreed statements (B)*		*No response Statements*	*Total (A+B) C_1*	*χ^2 value = $\Sigma \frac{(O-E)^2}{E}$ (A_1)*	*χ^2 value = $\Sigma \frac{(O-E)^2}{E}$ (B_1)*
Observed Freq. (O)	*Expctd. Freq.(E)*	*Observed Freq. (O)*	*Expctd. Freq.(E)*				
80	51.21	16	44.79	4	96	16.185	18.505
60	50.67	35	44.33	5	95	1.717	1.963
40	52.27	58	45.73	2	98	2.880	3.292
45	50.67	50	44.33	5	95	0.634	0.725
55	51.74	42	45.26	3	97	0.205	0.234
60	51.74	37	45.26	3	97	1.318	1.507
35	52.81	64	46.19	1	99	6.006	6.867
45	53.34	55	46.66	0	100	1.304	60.976
30	51.74	67	45.26	3	97	9.134	10.442
40	51.74	57	45.26	3	97	2.663	3.045
45	52.27	53	45.73	2	98	1.011	1.155
80	51.21	16	44.79	4	96	16.185	18.505
70	51.74	27	45.26	3	97	6.444	7.366
50	52.81	49	46.19	1	99	0.149	0.170
65	50.67	30	44.33	5	95	4.052	4.632
45	53.34	55	46.66	0	100	1.304	60.976
48	52.27	50	45.73	2	98	0.348	0.398
55	51.21	41	44.79	4	96	0.280	0.320
60	52.81	39	46.19	1	99	0.978	1.119
55	52.27	43	45.73	2	98	0.1425	0.162
35	50.67	60	45.33	5	95	4.846	5.539
40	53.34	60	46.66	0	100	3.336	60.976
45	51.74	52	45.26	3	97	0.877	1.330
70	51.74	27	45.26	3	97	6.444	7.366
55	52.27	43	45.73	2	98	0.142	0.162
40	52.81	59	46.19	1	99	3.107	3.552
50	51.21	46	44.79	4	96	0.028	0.032
55	50.67	40	44.33	5	95	0.370	0.422
T_1 1453	T_2 1271				T_3 2724	Total of (A_1+B_1) χ^2 = 373.529	

Source: Data collected through questionnaire.

Note: No response statements have been excluded while calculating c^2 value.

V = (r-1) x (c-1)

= (28-1) x (2-1)

= 27

Expected frequency = $(T_1 \times C_1) / T_3$

where r refers to rows and c refers to columns.

χ^2 (calculated value) = 373.53

$\chi^2_{0.05, 27}$ = 40.113 (table value)

The calculated value of c^2 is much greater than the table value, hence the hypothesis H_0 (null hypothesis) is rejected and H_1 (alternative hypothesis) is accepted.

Thus, the result of experiment does not support the hypothesis. Therefore the researcher concludes that factors framed affect the overall improvement of the functioning of Air Sahara.

TABLE 6.4

JET AIRWAYS

Chi-square Value

Agreed statements (A)		*Disagreed statements (B)*		*No response Statements*	*Total (A+B) C_1*	*χ^2 value = $\Sigma \frac{(O-E)^2}{E}$ (A_1)*	*χ^2 value = $\Sigma \frac{(O-E)^2}{E}$ (B_1)*
Observed Freq. (O)	*Expctd. Freq.(E)*	*Observed Freq. (O)*	*Expctd. Freq.(E)*				
90	59.43	8	38.57	2	98	15.724	24.229
65	57.61	30	37.39	5	95	0.947	1.459
55	60.04	44	38.96	1	99	0.422	0.651
50	60.04	49	38.96	1	99	1.678	2.586
45	60.64	55	39.36	0	100	4.036	93.431
55	60.64	45	39.36	0	100	0.525	93.451
40	58.83	57	38.17	3	97	6.024	9.283
60	60.04	39	38.96	1	99	2.472	3.811
75	60.04	24	38.96	1	99	3.728	5.745
55	58.83	42	38.17	3	97	0.248	0.383
65	58.22	31	37.78	4	96	0.789	1.217
60	58.83	37	38.17	3	97	0.023	0.036

55	58.43	43	38.57	2	98	0.330	0.509
70	59.43	28	38.57	2	98	1.879	2.895
55	57.61	40	37.39	5	95	0.118	0.152
65	59.43	33	38.57	2	98	0.521	0.903
40	60.04	59	38.96	1	99	66117.4	10206
80	59.43	18	38.57	2	98	7.118	10.968
60	58.83	37	38.17	3	97	0.023	0.036
50	57.61	45	37.39	5	95	1.005	1.550
40	58.83	57	38.17	3	97	6.024	9.283
55	58.83	42	38.17	3	97	0.248	0.383
70	58.83	27	38.17	3	97	2.122	3.270
45	58.22	51	37.78	4	96	3.001	4.625
55	58.83	42	38.17	3	97	0.248	0.383
T_1	T_2				T_3	Total of $(A_1+B_1)\ \chi^2$	
1655	1073				2728	= 380.804	

Source: Data collected through questionnaire.

Note: No response statements have been excluded while calculating χ^2 value.

V = (r-1) x (c-1)

Column = 2, rows = 28

= (2-1) x (28-1)

= 27 x 1 = 27

Expected frequency = $(T_2 \times C_1) / T_3$

where r refers to rows and c refers to columns.

χ^2 (calculated value) = 380.80

$\chi c^2_{0.05,\ 27}$ = 40.113 (table value)

Since the calculated value of c^2 is much more than the table value, hence the hypothesis H_0 (null hypothesis) is rejected and H_1 (alternative hypothesis) is accepted.

Thus, the result of experiment does not support the hypothesis. Hence, the researcher concludes that factors framed affect the overall improvement of the functioning of Jet Airways.

Keeping in view the objectives of the study, respondents' opinion regarding the Human Resource Planning in Air Sahara and Jet Airways have been presented and analysed in Tables 6.3 & 6.4. It is evident that majority of the employees agree with the statements of questionnaire that human resource planning is to be considered as an extremely important factor for productivity. The majority (80% in case of Air Sahara & 90% in case of Jet Airways) of the respondents agree with the same. It shows that opinion of the respondents is not equally distributed. It can be concluded that they feel that the top management do not belief that human resource planning is must for every dynamic tourism organization. Tables also show that a few respondents are uncertain about their opinions regarding various statements of questionnaire.

Most of the employees feel that there is need to re-structure their organizations, plan, train and develop the human resources according to its pre-determined objectives. They feel that their potentialities are not identified and fully utilized for enhancing productivity of both the organizations. While HRP has been helping Air Sahara and Jet Airways, the overall performance as regards higher productivity has not been so encouraging. The main reason is conflict between employees and the top management in the organization which leads to strike and unrest among the employees. Further, organisational culture created within the organizations are not conducive for sustainable development.

In the context of domestic business tourism, India largely, depends upon Indian Airlines. But the quality of services of Indian Airlines are not quite satisfactory. Hence, the people has started moving towards the private domestic carriers.

From time to time, there have been rumours of a cash strain, but no real data has ever emerged either on the group or any of its companies. Now, for the first time, documents available with TOI suggest that Air Sahara, the group's high-profile airline, is facing a degree of financial strife.

The airline has an accumulated loss of Rs. 100 crore and is likely to end the year with a loss of Rs. 118 crore in its books.

Air Sahara is expected to report a net loss of Rs. 17 crore for the current financial year, as against a profit of Rs. 32 crore last year.

These figures were extracted from a report that Ernst and Young had recently prepared for Air Sahara to help it raise capital either through a strategic investor or a private equity firm. Despite this, E&Y has valued Sahara at somewhere between $750 million $1 billion. It's expecting a strategic investor to bring in at least $100 million translating into a maximum 14% stake if one were to go by the $1 billion valuation.

With a strategic investor on board, Air Sahara hopes to raise Rs. 2,703 crore of debt. This will enable the airline to expand its fleet by another 15 Boeing 737-800 aircraft and also hire expensive pilots.

It may be concluded that accumulated losses have hit Rs. 100 cr and likely to jump to Rs. 118 cr. By year-end. Losses to touch Rs. 17 cr for the current year from a Rs. 32 or profit in the last year. CEO blames lack of pilots for poor utilization of fleet. Hopes for better show later this year. Looking for a strategic investor to infuse $100 million for a marginal stake.[1]

According to the agreement, both the airlines had agreed to conclude the $500-million (Rs. 2,300 crore) deal by March 24. but as certain clearances are still awaited from the government, the final transaction has not been completed and the airlines are contemplating extending the final date for concluding deal.

To conclude data in a meaningful manner and to find out the perceptions and opinions Chi-square (c^2) test is used in the tables 6.3 & 6.4. There are 28 parameters in these table which measures these opinions effectively. Statistically there is no difference between the expected and the observed frequencies. According to the results of chi-square, it is observed that the calculated c^2 values for these 28 variables are greater than the table value (Table value of Chi-square for 2, $c^2_{0.05} = 40.113$) and are significant at 0.05 percent level of significance. Thus the hypothesis Ho is rejected and H_1 (alternative hypothesis) is accepted. Hence there is a significant difference among respondents over the opinion about HRP in Tourism sector in India. Therefore, the researcher concludes that the factors framed affect the overall improvement of the functioning of Air Sahara and Jet Airways.

The next chapter highlights Summary of Findings, Conclusions, and make pragmatic and practical Suggestions and Recommendations.

REFERENCES

1. Hardasmalani, Datta Rumi and Sinha Prabhakar, "Sahara trying to woo domestic suitors", *The Times of India*, New Delhi, dated October 24, 2005, p. 10.
2. "Pilots jittery as jet snaps up Air Sahara", *Times of India*, 20 Jan. 2006.
3. "Jet-Sahara deal hits air pocket", *Times of India*, New Delhi, March 22, 2006.
4. "Jet-Sahara deal under MRTPC lens", *The Times of India*, New Delhi, March 2, 2006, p. 8.
5. "Over Rs. 100 cr. Losses for Air Sahara", *Times of India*, October 23, 2005.
6. Byas Anand, "Jet all set to take over Air Sahara", *Times of India*, New Delhi, January 12, 2006.
7. 'Government clears transfer of Air Sahar assets to Jet', The Times of India, dated 31.3.06, New Delhi, p. 10.
8. Hardasmalani, Datta Rumi and Sinha Prabhakar, "The truth's out: Air Sahara is bleeding", *The Times of India*, New Delhi, October 24, 2005, p. 1.

7

Conclusion

From the statistical analysis and interpretation made in the previous chapter it is inferred that majority of the respondents agree with the opinion that top management needs to assess regularly the surplus and shortage of human resources considering the needs of the ITDC for present and future requirements. Employees are not satisfied with the efforts made by the management to determine levels of future recruitment and selection needs.

The majority of the respondents do not have the same opinion over the issue of determination of future training and management development of ITDC. It is notable that a majority of the respondents are uncertain over the issues and thus they are not satisfied with the provisions of controlling of wage and salary costs.

The majority of the respondents do not agree with the provisions related to ensuring optimum utilization of human resources employed considering the ITDC requirements.

Further, majority of the respondents are uncertain regarding provision of a basis for future management development programmes. Thus, they are not satisfied with this issue.

The analysis of the statistical tools also leads to the conclusion that ITDC is lacking in laying emphasis on making efforts to meet the needs of expansion and diversification programmes.

The majority of the respondents disagree with the full development of human resource information system of ITDC.

As far as respondents' attitude towards slow growth of productivity in ITDC is concerned, they do agree with the statement.

Majority of the employees are not satisfied with unplanned Human Resource Planning leads to poor productivity.

The majority of the employees are disagree over the issue that poor planning leads to unencouraging profitability.

Respondents' opinion regarding Human Resource Planning in Air Sahara and Jet Airways have been presented and analysed and it is found that majority of the employees agree with the question of the questionnaire that the Human Resource Planning is must for every dynamic tourism organization. They feel that top management do not consider it seriously.

Most of the employees feel that there is need to re-structure the organizations of Air Sahara and Jet Airways and train, plan and develop them according to its pre-determined objectives. They feel that their potentialities are not fully utilized for enhancing productivity of both organizations. While HRP has been helping Air Sahara and Jet Airways, the overall performance as regards higher productivity has not been so encouraging. The main reason is the conflict between employees and the management which leads to strike and unrest among them.

Majority of the employees are not satisfied with any expenditure exercise made in planning and development of Human Resourceincreases the cost of Human Resourceand add less to profitability.

The airline industry is classified into six segments: Major, flag-carriers, cargo airlines, independents, low cost carriers (LCCs), regional, and leisure.

The majors are airlines which have annual revenues in excess of $2 billion; flag-carriers are the national airlines; regional are the niche airlines limited to certain geographical parts; LCCs are the new breed airlines operating point to point with lower costs; and leisure are the charter operators.

An analysis of the top 150 airlines reveals that the majors have more than two-thirds share of the airline business. Their average operating margin is negative 3.9 per cent in 2003, while that of the LCCs is much better at 6.9 per cent. The majors grew in 2003 by only 4.4 per cent while the LCCs expanded by 28 per cent. Thus, the LCCs have grown profitably in 2003, showing way for the majors.

The cost side of the airline business has deteriorated considerably, as carriers soak up increased ATF (airline turbine fuel) costs which are indexed to prices of crude oil. In 2004, as crude oil went up from $35 to $55 a barrel, few airlines had hedged against such price rise. As per International Air Transport Association (IATA) forecast, the airline industry losses in 2004 would be $4 billion, in spite of improved traffic, mainly due to rise in ATF costs.

Private Airlines in Asia Financially Better

Privately owned Asian airlines, such as Cathay Pacific and Singapore Airlines, always had good financial conditions due to stronger growth but the financials of US airlines are extremely poor.

Three of the leading airlines of the US among the Big Six – US Airways, United Airlines and Delta – recently filed for bankruptcy protection; most others with notable exception of Southwest, clearly demonstrate the difficulty faced by US carriers as they fight to cope with the changed operational and financial environment. The US majors can survive only if they successfully cut costs to meet long-term reduced revenues, and reduce debts by bringing in fresh capital.

Airlines in India Not Consistently Profitable Till 2003

The Government-owned Air India and Indian Airlines have been modest in their losses since the last five years. As per published financial results, Air India, India's international airline,

51st in 2003 in global rankings, in terms of revenue, had a negative operating margin on 2.6 per cent resulting in a loss of $ 33.3 million against a loss of $40.3 million in 2002.

Indian Airlines, ranked 73rd in 2003, with revenues $851 million, reported net losses of Rs. 196.5 crore in 2003, 246.75 crore in 2002, and 159.17 crore in 2001, as per the DGCA.

India's largest private airline, Jet Airways, globally ranked 94th with revenues of $595 million, was reported to have made a net loss of Rs. 244.5 crore, as per DGCA reports, in 2002-03, loss of Rs. 13.4 crore in 2001-02, and a profit of Rs. 12.4 crore in 2001, as per the DGCA, Air Sahara had a net loss of Rs. 37.75 crore in 2002-03, loss of Rs. 159.9 crore in 2001-02, and loss of Rs. 34.9 crore in 2000-01.

The boom in international arrivals, better financial performance of India Inc, and an increase in the incomes of IT professionals all contributed to a surge in domestic travel in 2004. Jet Airways recorded a net profit of Rs. 259 crore for the nine months period ended on December 31, 2004, as per company sources. Air Sahara and Indian Airlines are also expected to turn in better performances this year. As the competition in India is so far limited, the fares in domestic sectors are considerably higher than international fares.

Airline and Aviation Supply Chain

The aviation supply chain consists of airlines, airports, airline equipment manufacturers, airline IT suppliers (like GDS), travel agents and the traveller.

According to an analysis of top 150 airlines' profitability with that of airports, aircraft manufacturers, and IT suppliers, airlines have the most adverse profitability margins.

The new Director-General of IATA, has been complaining against monopoly airline suppliers such as air traffic controllers, airports, and GDS, IT vendors, aircraft manufacturers such as Boeing and Airbus, who benefit at the cost of airlines.

The main reasons why airlines are rarely profitable are:

- Highly capital intensive (with high fixed costs on aircraft, their maintenance, IT infrastructure, crew training, etc.) as well as labour intensive.
- Governments usually like to retain partial control of the airlines and hesitate in liberalizing ownership.
- Low profitability – deflationary revenues and inflationary costs.
- Cyclical nature with longer period of recession and shorter recovery.
- Strong influence of external environment whether economic, political or environment.
- Very few professionally managed.
- Complex pricing structures, restrictive conditions.
- Steep fall in demand for business travel, especially post 9/11.
- Reducing pricing power due to competition from LCCs.
- Escalating fuel prices, and
- Additional security and insurance charges after 9/11.

In the 1990s, liberalization of Indian skies saw a plethora of private airlines, such as Jet Airways, Damania Airways, East West Airlines, NEPC, UB Air and Archana Air taking to the skies.

However, most of these private airlines, with the exception of Jet Airways, have now ceased to exist. Varios factors account for the disappearance from scene of these airlines. It may be noted that private airlines were formed before the appropriate time or they might have to pay the price for not understanding the low profitability, high capital cost implicit in the airline business.

Now, with income levels rising in urban India, private airlines have better prospects. Close on the heels of the success of Air Deccan, India's first LCC, many private airlines such as Kingfisher airlines, rechristened from B Air; Royal Air, rechristened from

ModiLuft; and Eastwest airlines are readying to take off again, promising to bring down air fares and challenging the oligopoly of Indian Airlines and jet Airways. Moreover, with liberalization of bilaterals by the Ministry of Civil Aviation, the domestic private airlines such as Jet Airways and Air Sahara can now explore new horizons in the UK, Singapore, hitherto a preserve of Air India and Indian Airlines; with this development, the fortunes of the domestic airlines seem to be viewed in more favourable terms.

The industry's low profitability and its capital and intensivity, mean that airlines will struggle to earn profits, as forces of competition are unleashed.

Recently quite a few low-cost airlines in Europe such as Air Polonia (Polish), Volare (Italian), V-Bird (Dutch), Jet Magic (Irish) and Now and Duo (British) have gone bankrupt unable to sustain the cyclical pressures of the industry.

While the Indian air traveller looks forward to the launch of more airlines leading to more competition, lowering of airfares, the newly established airlines are advised to stay on course, by avoiding the air pockets of the airline business.[1]

The trend of travel to India is booming and is undoubtedly expected to grow continually in the coming years. However, some undermining factors become apparent, particularly during peak periods, which might have a negative effect and thus restrict further development of this trend.

- The network of Jet Airways services is often not sufficient to accommodate the demand on the most frequented tourist routes.
- he actual frequency of flights to some important destinations, the seat capacity offered and the operational standards have not always kept pace with the growth rate of air traffic.
- There is a shortage of air conditioned limousines and buses.
- The equipments being used at present often does not meet the international standards.

- The rates and fares charged by Jet Airways services are substantially high. In India, the rates charged by airlines are roughly ten times the rates charged by railway from second class passengers. It is therefore, a transport of rich and well-to-do tourist. It can not become a mass tourism. But there is need for a change towards the low cost Airline to came into existence.
- Inclement weather caused by storms, rains or fog restricts the transport flow. The bad weather is more harmful to aircraft journey. Therefore Air transport is a good weather friend and can not provide service in the rough weather. This results in unreliability and uncertainty of flight timings.
- Air transport miserably suffers from higher frequency and greater intensity of accidents. Most of the accident are fatal and survivors are rare. The accidents may be due to miscalculations on the part of pilot, failure of the machine fire crash against some high peak or buildings or inadequate training of the pilots. This restricts the use and operations.
- The ground service transporters like bus drivers tax drivers etc. charge heavily from the tourist, specially from an international tourist. This kind of practices hampers the image of country in the world tourism market.
- There are not many highways and planned roads to facilitate the transport. This is mainly due to inadequate financial assistance.
- In India the area of operations of air transport is very limited. The flights are few and infrequent and for a few places only. In India, airports are very few and are concentrated in big cities only.

In the context of domestic business tourism, India largely depends upon Indian Airlines. But the quality of services of Indian Airlines are not quite satisfactory. Hence, people have started moving towards the private domestic carriers.

It is believed that Ministry of Civil Aviation has failed in convincing the Finance Ministry for the very needed development of infrastructure. It is imperative on the part of the Department of Civil Aviation to fight all the way to acquire the resources required for integrated infrastructure development. Without this it would be impossible to gain for the growth and development of this very potential and strategic Indian Airlines and Air India Ltd.

Conclusion

Tourism is a human experience, a social experience, a geographical phenomenon, a resource value, and a business industry. It is a major social phenomenon of the modern society with enormous economic consequences. Its importance as an instrument for economic development and employment generation, particularly in remote and backward areas, has now been well recognized the world over. The industry today is globally recognized as a major economic contributor and employment generator. The investment flows into this field are constantly on the increase.

The developing countries must first develop the human resources in order to develop a tourism institutional structure in which technological innovation can occur on a large scale. Economic development can succeed only when the environment as a whole is conducive to change and innovation at all levels and on all fronts. This will require educated masses, literate and national masses.

The strategies supported to achieve the goal of human resources development in tourism industry include more open government, more transparent and accountable public administration and development of energetic entrepreneurship in developing countries and further liberalization of markets and goods, capital, technology and tourism products. This would require joint action programmes. A new vision for global co-operation for the next century is needed.

It has become imperative that tourism sector should concentrate on HRP system for grooming. HR in such a manner so as to flourish and achieve international competitiveness in tourism.

The tourism industry is faced with various challenges in the field of human resources. One of the crucial issues in this regard is the quality of Human Resource. The industry is vitally faced with the demand for qualified quality personnel.

The Government of India has shown some interest, though obviously not enough, in the promotion of tourism sector over the years, the Government has realized the importance of the skilled in the field at different level to plan, train and develop human resources.

There is still a strong potential for further growth rate in tourism to India and better transport services could play a dominant role in the overall development of tourism in India. It is observed that increases in tourism in the future would much depend on the successful handling of the areas, like by providing proper facilitation in travel formalities. The infrastructure problems should also be solved with an emphasis on transportation because there is an urgent need for attention to roads not only for national highways but also the rural and urban roads all over the country. Technological upgradation of vehicles is also necessary so that there inbuilt safety, driving comfort, fuel efficiency, reduced maintenance costs and greater reliability. Besides upgrading the technology Human Resource Planning should also be done for ensuring better driving and maintenances skills.

Human Resource Planning is a strategy for the acquisition, utilization, improvement and pressure on Human Resources. Human Resource Planning is the system, which ensures availability of new personnel in terms of quality and quantity as and when they are required. Thus, Human Resource Planning refers to establishing job specifications or the qualitative requirement of jobs and determining the number of people required, as per goals and objectives.

Today, Human Resource Planning (HRM) is considered as the way management comes to grasp the ill-defined and toughto-solve human resource problems facing an organization. The tools used in the process as well as the importance of the process depends on the problems being confronted by the management. The nature of the problems relates to broad external changes and issues inherent in corporate strategies and plans. The key to effective Human Resource Planning in the analysis of the factors representing change – change that potentially affects survival, growth, efficiency and effectiveness, as well as excellence, productivity and profitability of business.

No exaggeration, recruitment and selection is an important function of Human Resource Planning in the tourism industry. Slightest mistake will lead to ruin the whole tourism industry. The role of HR manager is very crucial in selecting and recruiting the right kind of people who can be an asset for the tourism sector. Instead of following a blind elimination process, focuss should be on selecting people based on the skills and competencies required for the job.

The training and development plans are aimed at developing talents to perform effectively in the present and future higher levels on more challenging work situations. The T&D activities are the techniques of encashing on the human capital whose potential is much more than any other resources in the organization. The rapid increase in the size of the organization and the technological advancement have resulted in delegating the authorities and responsibilities to the supervisors. This has added new dimensions to the role profile of a supervisor.

The latest approach of supervisory development takes into account his foresight, sympathetic approach, ability to suggest improvements in methods, develop understanding between management and workforce, strive for improvement, and so forth. He has to organize the work and manage the operations. The success of the department depends upon the supervisor. It calls for high standards of general ability, degree of intelligence, maturity of character and a temperament to control the shopfloor.

The success of an organization depends on its ability to affect continuous improvement and provide quality products and services to its customer. This will require every personnel in the organization to possess the requisite knowledge, skill and attitude. For the purpose of determining training requirements, two levels of supervision could be identified. Each level of supervision should have a curriculum that addresses competencies required at that level.

The role of training and development programmes is most essential as it helps not only in 'managing others', but in managing self and it inculcates among participants a feeling to aspire for higher and higher excellence and effectiveness and thereby increased productivity.

Suggestions

For a prosperous society, it is vitally important that productivity graph moves upward. No doubt, technological sophistication and industrial innovation result in higher productivity but the magnitude of success is influenced by efforts taken in the field of educational innovations. Professionalism without ethical excellence carries no meaning. Hence, an organization requires to develop technological expertise along with ethics and work attitude. This naturally diverts our attention on initiating qualitative improvements in the education and training facilities so that professional and inter-personal potentialities are developed.

An effective management recognizes that planning, training and development is an ongoing and continuous process, not a 'one-shot' activity. New problems, new procedures and equipments, new knowledge and new jobs are constantly creating the need for training and development. The justification for the investment of time, money, or any other resources in training and development activities is that it can contribute to the productivity and profitability of the enterprise. Training activities, properly planned, conducted and evaluated, help to raise the productivity of the tourism industry through the more effective use of human resources.

In order to manage change for productivity, organization members need to understand their own organisation's culture, and to see their own organization as a potentially flexible and dynamic system. Only then a vision of the future for productivity improvement can be developed and an appreciation of the route need to take to achieve that vision. In this climate of rapid change, it has become imperative for executives and managers to rethink their conventional approaches. The integrated committed culture comprising efficiency, flexibility and commitment may solve some of the issues which has resulted from the new challenges posed of new business environment.

Although the future of tourism transport will depend on the extent and pace of development of technology, yet it can be safely said that in the years to come it will play greater role and offer much greater services to tourism specially the air transport.

The role of Air Sahara and Jet Airways in the promotion of tourism in India can not be ignored but there is a need to bring some innovative changes in the management strategies for making the efforts meaningful. Air Sahara and Jet Airways play a very supportive role for tourism industry.

Further, to increase the tourist flow the Government has to pay attention to the air transport services like by improving the quality of services which its national carrier and international carrier provides to the tourist. It has to bring innovative changes in the marketing strategies for competing with competitors of this field. The Jet airways has to introduce tourism oriented schemes for attracting foreign tourist, for example, budget tours in off seasons, incentive tours etc. Besides this, it has to provide enough funds for the tourism publicity division and establish tourism cell in the big cities, appointing the full time tourism director in management body so that he could give suggestion how to improve the tourist attracting tactics.

If Jet Airways wants to have a stand in the market against its competitors then the carrier has to have better and effective publicity of its promotional schemes and better marketing strategies. To improve its market reputation it has to introduce extraordinary facilities and comfort on the flights on very reasonable fares. Efforts should be made to introduce new destinations which have the capacity to generate tourist traffic.

Air Sahara and Jet Airways play a very important role in tourism, both at the domestic and international level. It is abundantly clear that air transport plays a dominant role in the inter-regional movement of tourists, which normally entails travel over long distances and frequently over-water barriers as between, for example, North America and Europe. Again, air transport is also of growing importance in intra- regional travel where substantial distances are involved and geographical obstacles impede easy movement. The rate of growth of international air traffic has persisted at around 15 per cent a year, and this increased use of air transport by tourist is the result of a number of factors: people have become air travel-minded, travel is immeasurably quicker and fares have generally decreased. The most decisive development, however, has been the development of inclusive tours in which travellers are carries on charter flights at rates substantially below those of normal scheduled services.

Role of transport in the context of Indian tourism industry is indispensable and one could say that the rail transport, road transport, water transport and air transport have made a considerable contribution in promoting the tourism in the country specially the air transport has played a dominant role in bringing more and more international tourist to the country and facilitating the domestic tourist who have money but no time to spend on unnecessary time consuming modes of transport.

India is too far away from the main tourist generating centres of the world both in the west like US and Europe and in the east Japan and Korea. Thus, making it quite a bit expensive for most down market tourists from these centres wanting to get here, while the rich travellers of the Indian subcontinent prefer western destinations instead. The other constraint being high hotel tariffs in metropolitan cities.

No clear cut transport Government policy, poor capitalization from new investors, inadequate airport infrastructure outside metros are some of the factors responsible for slow growth and poor performance of civil aviation industry.

There is a need for proper and liberal aviation policy from the Government which encourages charters and other international carriers wanting to touch India, while at the same time provide adequate incentives for development of domestic civil aviation both in private and public sectors.

Delays in clearance of private airline and airport development proposals, restrictive tax rules for Government servants getting family leave travel allowance (LTA) and wanting to travel by air are hampering the development of civil aviation in the country. Government should amend tax laws pertaining it easier for families, who want to travel by air.

Expensive aviation turbine fuel (ATF), mounting overheads etc. have forced many private airlines to tighten their purse strings, while others have been taken over. Though Government has allowed import of small aircraft for short haul routes, they remain unattractive as compared to trunk routes in spite of competition, costs and almost stagnant market base.

The tourist market has been characterized up to now by a very high price elasticity of demand. IUOTO (now WTO) puts the coefficient of elasticity at about 1.5 to 2.0. Therefore a reduction of 10% in air fares would lead to growth of 17 to 22% in traffic.

Private airlines started in India after the initiative taken by Government to launch the open sky policy. Initially they were called Air Taxis but later on they got the status of scheduled Airlines. The need of the hour is that Government makes necessary amendment in the Air Corporation Act 1953, to control and create the healthy competition between them and also to give permission to private Airlines to operate International flights from India because this will help in promoting Tourism in India, thereby making valuable contribution in the foreign exchange earnings of the country. It helps people in distress by reaching them long distances within a short time. Although from the point of view of volume of traffic, the role of air transport in the country's transportation system is insignification, except in the case of international passenger traffic, its value from the point of the quality of its service and the clientele it serves is very important. It also helps in the supply of essential supplies to hilly and inaccessible areas where no other means of communication. In the international field, air transport has helped in developing trade with other nations. With the faster development of passengers, major cities of the world have come nearer to each other.

In the field of international tourism, airport plays a very important role. Because all the Airlines operates from Airports. The Government should take necessary steps for the modernization of the Airports and to build Airports in those cities which either do not have or have excess load on the existing ones. Tourism is one of the largest single element in international trade for contributes significantly to the nation' earnings. Developing airline services and offering attractive air-fares have largely contributed to the success of world tourism. It is estimated that 85% of the foreign tourists arrive in India by air. The relative decline of air fares has made international air tourism increasingly attractive and as a result tourists arrival in India have shown remarkable increase. According to a survey 80% of those who come to India by air, like to travel within the country also by air. To meet the demands of growing traffic, the fleet of the two national carriers – Indian Airlines and Air India, were expanded and equipped with modern jet aircrafts.

Air traffic rights in international sectors are arranged bilaterally between countries. Air services are either scheduled or non-scheduled. On scheduled services, it is possible to travels as an independent passenger, as an inclusive tour passenger (individually or in a group), as an excursion fare paying passenger or as a member of an affinity charter group. Fare structures are calculated, following a chart of normal fares, circle trip fares, G.I.T. fares, IT fares, or special distinguished areas. On unscheduled services, it is impossible to travels as a charter inclusive tour passenger as a member of an affinity charter group or a member of a split charter group. The IATA (International Air Transport Authority) is the body that fix international fares of member airlines. The interdependence of tourism and aviation is an indisputable fact. Improved airline services and promotion fares attract an ever increasing number of tourists. Air transport depends on tourist traffic to a great extent for their revenue and therefore makes strenuous efforts in promoting tourism.

ITDC provides leadership and promote high quality tourism brand for India by achieving high level of excellence and profit in the field of hotels, tour and travel, duty free shops, Human Resource Planning and consultancy and creating tourism infrastructure as well as foreign partnership with State Government for undertaking tourism projects.

The declining profits of ITDC are owing to the interference of the Government which gives a blow to the functioning of different parts of the organization, be it recruitment and promotion of employees, changing marketing strategies, venturing into new areas, financial prospects or other prospects of the organization. Each and every decision of the organization has to be approved by the Government. This does not give much chance of innovation and initiative of the managers. The management is reduced merely to application of ideas of the top level decision makers. Perhaps this is the reason why ITDC lags behind its counterparts.

"The persons sitting at the decision making table in the Government are no experts in tourism. They do not understand the problems faced by a Service Industry, most importantly, the industry dealing with leisure activities".[2]

The fact is that government only realised the benefit of tourism and the immense potential in the area. And ITDC is the only public sector organization working for the promotion of tourism in India, and thus faces problems.

Day to day interference by the government machinery causes hindrance to the working environment, and also delays several important projects. The priority of work shifts its focus on the government's demands and decisions with haphazard growth of tourism in India and equally unmindful policies of government regarding tourism pose a big threat for the organization that takes initializing for development of this growing industry.

All the public sector organization are formed with the sole purpose of development of infrastructure, with no particular initiative for profit and ITDC is not far behind.

This is the reason why ITDC keeps on trying new concepts, where private sector dare not enter. On the other hand, this is the reason why ITDC suffers losses. Tourism Task Force; the concept provided by ITDC, was a project of great innovation, but also greatly initiated. Camps were established and all modern facilities were used, but it would not cope up with the budget constraints, and has to be closed down. This also caused unnecessary diversion of resources.

Secondly, lots of investment and resources of ITDC are wasted for the development of infrastructure in the areas which are not profitable from business point of view. If all these resources had to be judiciously used in developing those areas which brought good returns on investment, all the funds and Human Resourcewould have gone for a better use.

> "In the case of ITDC the principles of Cost-Benefit Analysis does not work. Any losses due to the inconsistent government policies, unstable political and law and order situations, and many other which affect this sensitive industry have to be borne by the organization without grudges. And the result of this is that the organisation feels that it can bear any amount of losses, as government is always there to take it out of difficulties. If such is the feeling of the only government organization in this developing industry, the fate of the whole tourism industry is just anybody's guess".[3]

For the generation of profit the ITDC should establish effective coordination with all the relevant agencies so as to achieve synergy in the development of tourism. The ITDC should concentrate on a few selected centres and circuits to achieve balanced development of infrastructure in an integrated manner.

ITDC should plan hotel projects in the newly created State of Uttranchal which is now becoming a desirable spot for adventure lovers. New trekking routes are being developed. ITDC can plan budget hotels in this area and also assist in transport facilities.

"There are many restricted protected areas in North-East States, Lakshadweep and Andaman & Nicobar Islands. Special tourist permits are necessary for visiting these areas. Due to lesser tourists visiting these areas, private sector is hesitant to invest here. ITDC should take initiative to build lodges and resorts in these areas.

Further there are many hidden treasures in India, like the cool, scheduled beaches in Goa, hill stations, lesser known monuments and other architectural wonders, which needs proper infrastructural development. One area which ITDC has not explored is the new concept of tourism, i.e., Adventure Tourism. This form of tourism not only requires knowledge but also huge investment in the modern equipments. ITDC should denote a separate department for exploring the potentials of Adventure Tourism in India"

And finally, ITDC has tremendous potential for Convention Tourism with the back drop of excellent infrastructure necessary for a convention or symposium, and years of experience. ITDC can pool all its resources and make a separate department of conventions. The Convention Wing in Marketing Division and that of Ashok Travels and Tours should be combined, and both should work together.

The fact is that ITDC has a large potential of growth in the coming years. What is required is a systematically and coordinated effort, to bring, all units together, as an opportunity to India.

Sahara and Jet Airways should give preference to quality of services if it is planning to go international since most of the passengers give priority to the airlines providing good quality of services. It includes both in-flight services and ground services.

Sahara and Jet Airways should observe on time operation of flights and punctuality in schedule.

Time to time introduction of various discounted fare schemes for excursionists, economy class and even business class passengers are also conducive to growth of tourism. Since Delhi-London is one of the costliest route in terms of air travelling and discounted fares definitely will fascinate the passengers.

Discounted fares scheme for students should be made available during the beginning and end of academic sessions of various British and Indian Universities.

To enter a new market Sahara and Jet Airways should keep its fares for each class similar to the fares of CIS carriers but should give services that European carrier are giving. As a result it will fascinate more and more passengers.

During the high season Sahara and Jet Airways may increase the fares a bit to cover the cost of operation and during the low season they should allow discounts to fascinate passengers, since mobility of passengers during low season is low and discounted fares may attract a few more towards Sahara.

Sahara being a new international airline should operate twice a week to maintain economic operation otherwise airline will go down in terms of financial status due to over cost.

As far as the configuration of seats is concerned Sahara and Jet Airways should allow more seats to economy class and excursion class in the beginning since it is pretty easy to fascinate economy class and excursionists towards a new airline through discounted fares and other schemes while business class traveller doesn't rely upon new airlines easily, since they are very particular about time and convenience.

A major condition for HRP to succeed is that it should be seen as an integral part of every manager's role and not merely as the body of the personnel department. So far, managers have been expecting the personnel departments to take the primary responsibility for planning, identifying and developing human resources.

The main suggestions to make HRP effective in tourism sector in India are as under:

- There should be an explicit corporate policy on Human Resource Planning.

- The top head must have full belief in the value of his employees who are his greatest resource.
- HRP needs of the tourism organization should be seriously planned, examined and an action plan for HRP should be prepared.
- HRP departments should be headed by competent persons and should be placed close to the Chief Executive on the organization chart.
- Conducive climate should be developed in the tourism industry.
- Heads of various departments who are dealing with HRP should be encouraged to share their experiences and develop professionally the human resource under them.
- It is the right time to accord the status of priority to tourism industry due to increase in tourist arrivals and the socio-economic benefits of the tourism phenomenon.
- The Government should set up a high power committee consisting of Human Resource Planning professionals, professionals from the tourism industry, prominent economists and intellectuals to study and assess various aspects of HRP and conclude on a National Tourism Policy on HRP.
- Tourism which is a highly labour intensive industry, should have an integrated HRP system with both public and private sector participation in order to develop human resources to meet the requirements of tourism industry.
- Human Resourceresource division of Public and Private sector organizations should look that programmes for HRP are conducted with foreign collaborations for maintaining International status.
- In this modern age, the planners technologies are exposed to the tourism personnel for optimum efficiency and customer satisfaction.

- The training establishments/institutes should have exchange programme for personnel with foreign countries to ensure qualitative and quantitative training in successive development of human resource.
- Zonal Human Resourceresource centre should be established to recognize tourism as a factor for regional development and also should conduct studies on the availability of skilled and semi-skilled human resources in their concerned regions.
- In order to study the various training establishments and training programmes conducted by different countries, the perspective planners should send study missions for gathering information which will be useful in formulating plans and strategies for Human Resource Planning and setting up training establishments in our country.
- To choose the best human resource from various educational institutions/universities, we should incorporate vocational training programmes in order to create human resource from the grass root level. There should be awareness programmes and career orientation lectures to encourage youth to opt for career in the different segments of the tourism industry.
- A Parliamentary Affairs Committee should look into introducing Education Reform Bills to ensure quality education with an industrial approach and thereby develop human resources to a great extent.
- HRP programmes should give due emphasis on high tech functional training to impart necessary skills.
- Seminars, workshops, conferences should be conducted to discuss problems and prospects of HRP at the national and international level.
- For awareness and the implementation of various schemes for HRP, there should be a Confederation of Indian Travel Industries (CITI). The CITI can monitor the implementation and advise the Government in formulation

of policies for the development of the tourism industry in general and HRP in particular.

- A single-window facility for the tourists to avail of various services should be provided for promoting tourism in every state.
- Government should allow tax holidays for the hotels constructed in the remote areas and hill stations soon to boost tourist traffic.
- The hotels should make all arrangements to provide food to the tourists according to their tastes and linkages and this would give boost to tourism development in our country.
- The staff in the government holds are inefficient and fail to offer services of required standard. There must be a committee to investigate the complaints reported by the tourists and action should be taken against the employees who are found negligent on their part. They should be given orientation lectures and training programmes and even after that they are found incorrigible, should be replaced with polite and courteous staff.
- ITDC hotels need marketing and sales promotion which is largely lacking off at present.
- The reason for low occupancy rate of ITDC hotels should be identified and the discrepancies causing the low occupancy rate must be removed.
- More duty free shops should be added to the ITDC elite hotels.
- Red tapism, bureaucracy and politicians inferences should be avoided in hotels.
- Hospitality industry should employ skilled staff to provide extensive personal services. A well trained highly flexible staff is the hotel's most profitable investment.
- There should be decontrol of hotel tariff. Electricity, import license and other infrastructural facilities should be made available at concessional rates.

- The ITDC should use the time spent by travellers at airports offering an international shopping experience.
- There should be an arcade at the duty free shops that should sell only 'destination goods'. At the arcade the duty free shops should keep an array of Indian handicrafts, jewellery and handlooms.
- ITDC should tap the inbound traffic with glamour around shops.
- The State Governments should give priorities in regard to tourist attractions for overseas marketing.
- The India's tourism policy must focus on operational constraints which have hampered Indian tourism on a large scale.
- High taxation by the Government has resulted in lesser growth and development of Indian tourism. The State and Central Governments have levied taxes so heavily that India as a destination has become very expensive and unattractive to foreign tourists. The taxes which foreign tourists pay are expenditure tax, luxury tax, sales tax, charged by hotels, road tax, passenger tax, toll tax charged by the State Governments, airport department tax and on top of that the service tax. A new tourism policy should be drafted soon where those should be incorporation of relaxation on all these taxes.
- Indian tourism has not been coming on top to its potential level for the reason that the policies laid down by the Government are not conducive to the growth of international tourism in India. The travel segment is of the view that the travel industry hardly gets any benefits from the Government, except u/s 80 HHD of the Income Tax Act where 50 per cent of the income earned in foreign exchange is exempted.
- Inadequate infrastructure is another factor of much concern for Indian tourism. As a matter of fact, one of the major setbacks that the Department of Tourism has suffered is that its demand for substantial investments amounting

to Rs. 45,000 crores which involves Centre, State financial institutions and private sector to develop tourist infrastructure has remained unsatiated. Modernisation of Delhi and Mumbai airports is needed urgently. It s believed that the Department of Tourism has been unable to convince the Finance Ministry and the Planning Commission to grant adequate resources for the development of infrastructure. It is imperative on the part of the Department of Tourism to fight all the way to acquire those sources for integrated infrastructure development.

- Air Sahara should not be merged with Jet Airways. Rather it should compensate the previous losses by developing its infrastructure facilities on the international level, customers satisfaction and enhancing its number of fleets and so on.

Recommendations

In sum and substance the study finds that Human Resource Planning is gaining much attention from human resource specialists, academicians and employees alike. It is felt that the importance of HRP will increase further. As per forecast of World Tourism Organisation, tourism growth prospects for India are very bright and tourist arrivals and receipts are likely to increase fastly in the coming years. With these growing trends in the tourism industry in India which is considered labour intensive industry. Human resource plays an important role in managing, operating, planning and promoting tourism industry. Thus, HRP efforts in tourism industry needs a major transformation in the attitudes, behaviour and values of employees as well as management. This is possible only if appropriate organsiation culture is developed by the tourism organization to make HRP more successful and introduced it as a total system within the tourism industry.

Therefore, HRP plays a major role for the development of tourism sector. HRP should be taken on a priority basis and adequate planning measures should be undertaken accordingly because the best and efficient human resources can increase customer satisfaction and thereby to create a competitive edge in this global world. The customer satisfaction through HRP in tourism will continue to be a significant factor in determining how tourism develops in future. Effective customer care is more significant than training of the staff in smiling pleasant manner and complaint handling. Good customer relations come from a total management culture within an organization.

In spite of the fact that tourism has been given the status of an industry in India, inbound tourism or domestic tourism has not grown in planned manner. The reason is that govt. department. The hotel industry and the tour operators have no close cooperation or coordination among themselves. Further the role of the travel media has been completely ignored unlike any other country. Travel media plays an important role in giving an exposure to the best tourists products of a country the services of the travel industry and the good hotels/properties. Travel media is a guide for consumers as well as for the industry and the tour operators should make full use of it.

One of India's biggest problems is to find employment for its citizens. India has the largest number of unemployed persons in the world. Germany has about 0.45 million unemployed, the USA has about 8 million jobless people. The corresponding figure for India is 38 million. Travel and Tourism directly creates employment opportunities in hotels, airlines, travel agencies, passenger ships, transport companies, tour operation units, immigration, etc., and in industries like construction, money changing, telecommunication, souvenir shops, manufacturing and retail trade, as a result of the spread effect. Most important from India's point of view is the fact that these employment opportunities will be created in the small and medium segments of the industries and dispersed throughout the country. In India, travel and tourism is still considered an elite 'five star' activity, though WTO has recognized the role of this sector in poverty alleviation by job creation. We also need to note that tourism will be the leading job creator in the next decade, in the global economy.

It is evident that there is a need to strengthen the partnership between Government and the Industry to promote tourism education in India. The private sector should contribute in a big way to promote Education and Training for this critical sector, which is poised to grow tremendously in the new millennium. There is a need for greater collaboration between Government and the industry. Governments, whether at national or state levels, should adopt a leadership role in the development of human resources. They should facilitate urgent investment in education and training.

Another significant step to be taken is to bridge the gap between educational authorities and the industry – creating groups to develop the skills required by the industry. They should help promote careers in travel and tourism to help stimulate interest in the industry as a source of employment. Time and again, the need to set up an effective platform of body to take care of the interests of all the players of tourism has been put forth not only by scholars but also by the industry and opinion makers. Today the need for such a body is all the more crucial from the point of view of tourism training and education. Only such a body can make the industry realize its responsibilities towards tourism education and training. It is essential to advance the value of education and training in tourism to employers, employees and the Government. Unless all the players of tourism realize the importance of training and education nothing substantial can be achieved. A synergistic view of commitment towards Human Resource Planning is the key to success of the Travel and Tourism industry today as also in the years to come.

If the suggestions made are implemented properly, it will keep the ship of tourism sector sailing in the right direction. Without quality improvement in Human Resource Planning, the potential for development of tourism would be externally limited and the dream of achieving global competitiveness in the tourism sector will be in vain.

Main findings which have been drawn from the case studies

undertaken of Air Sahara and Jet Airways and ITDC which reveal that the factors affect the overall improvement of the functioning of Air Sahara and Jet Airways, and thus the strong recommendation is made to the Ministry of Civil Aviation and Ministry of Tourism, Government of India, New Delhi, to implement the suggestions for the proper functioning of these organizations and thereby maximize the profit as well as to achieve the desired results.

Demand for air seats between metros is growing fast as people have begin to attach value to time, but impediments in the way of expansion are inadequate ground handling and navigational facilities on these trunk routes. It is recommended that investment should be made to develop them.

The Jet Airways has done a lot in the field of tourism promotion in recent decades like giving more new promotional schemes and there by providing the incentives to the passengers or the tourists under various promotional schemes. It is also recommended that still it needs more attention towards promotion of tourism in India and abroad.

It is further recommended that the Government of India should form a 'HRP Board' which should encourage the researches upon increasing potentiality of human resources. It should take many productive and aggressive steps for the promotion of HRP. The need of the hour is to tackle grassroots realities of HRP and then take some harsh measures to infuse a new blood in Indian tourism sector.

Direction for Future Research

The study has elaborately dwelt upon Human Resource Planning instrumentalities in terms of planning, recruitment, selection, training and development, reward systems, performance appraisal, career development and counselling and organizational culture and effectiveness in tourism industry particularly referring to hospitality and service sector. Further research can be undertaken to study the tourism industry with reference to HRP in travel agencies and training institutes.

REFERENCES

1. Pandit, Pankaj Narayan "Airlines are rarely profitable", *Business Line*, New Delhi, Feb. 18, 2005.
2. Negi, J.M.S. (1998), *Travel and Tourism*, Geetanjali Publishing House, New Delhi, p. 390.
3. PTI Report, The Times of India, New Delhi, 12.10.1999, p. 6.

APPENDIX–IV

SAHARA AIRLINES – COMPANY PROFILE

Sahara Airlines	:	Established on 3rd December 1993 with one being 737-200
Chairman	:	Mr. Subrata Roy Sahara
Present Fleet	:	2 Being 737-800
	:	1 Being 737-700
	:	4 Being 737-400
	:	2 Being 737-200
	:	2 Ecuriel Helicopters
	:	2 Dauphin Helicopters
Objectives	:	To create a dependable and a professional airlines.
	:	To offer more value for money to its customers with international standards of services.
	:	To get a better market share.
	:	To earn foreign currency
	:	Creating meaningful flier programme
	:	Targeting at corporate traveler who is looking for a reliable airline performing on time.
Future Plan	:	Sahara is soon to induct the smaller aircraft to connect passengers to various cities other than metros.
Command Office	:	Sahara India Bhawan Kapoorthala Complex, Lucknow-226020

Corporate Office	:	7th Floor, Ambadeep Building, 14, K.G. Marg, New Delhi 110001 India
Reservation Systems	:	Gabriel II (Co-host), Amadeus, Abacus, Galileo, Sabre, Worldspan.
IATA	:	Member effective June 1996
IATA Clearing House Membership	:	Member effective 1st October 1996
Three Digit Designator	:	705
Staff	:	Over 1762 highly qualified experienced and dedicated staff including 95 pilots, 124 Flight crew, 72 engineers, 104 technician and 1366 ground staff.
Hubs of Operation	:	Delhi, Mumbai, Chennai
Engineering Base	:	Delhi (Hanger space of 32000 sq.ft.)
Cargo Capacity	:	Three tons per flight
Seat Factor	:	79% in peak season and 68% in low season.
Distribution Network	:	Through IATA Agents, through Sahara Airlines appointed agents, through GSAs through Interline partners.
	:	World Travel Market' 1997 Global award for its quality of service.
	:	Award of Merit on 8th May 1999.
	:	On Board service Diamond Award for excellence in food service at on 13th November 1999.
Interline Agreements	:	53 major international airlines.
GAS's	:	18 GSA's worldwide USA, UAE, Nepal, Srilanka
Tariff	:	Comparable with Indian Airlines
Type of Service	:	Both Business & Economy class

Source: Annual Report, Sahara Airlines, Sahara India Bhawan, Kapoorthala Complex, Lucknow, p. 110.

APPENDIX–V

SHARA FLEET OF AIRCRAFT

S2 has a fleet size of Nine Boeing Aircraft

- Two Boeing 737-800
- One Boeing 737-700
- Four Boeing 737-400
- Two Being 737-200

Type	*Seat Cap. (J/Y)*	*Seat Pitch (J/Y)*	*Intro Service*	*Fuel Cap.*	*Range Kg.*	*A/C Hours*
B-838-400	12/138	43/30-35	Nov.94	16,262	7	SIC
B-737-400	12/126	37/31	Dec.94	16,262	7	SID
B-337-200	8/101	37/31	Dec.96	15,688	6	*SIE
B-737-200	8/101	37/31	Jan.97	15,688	6	*SIF
B-737-700	12/114	38/30	May 99	20,896	9	SIG
B-737-400	24/112	43/30-35	Aug. 99	16,262	7	SIH
B-737-400	24/112	43/30-35	Dec.99	16,262	7	SII
B-737-800	12/156	38/31	Dec. 99	20,896	9	SIJ
B-737-800	12/156	38/31	Dec.99	20,896	9	SIK

*Owned by Sahara Airlines.

Average age of S2 fleet 7.9 Years.

Source: Field Survey.

APPENDIX–VI

THE JET AIRWAYS FLEET

AIRCRAFT	NUMBER OF SERVICE
BOEING 737-800	13
BOEING 737-700	11
BOEING 737-400	8
ATR 72-500	8
TOTAL NO.	40
AVERAGE AGE	3

THE FLEET FACTS

BOEING 737-800

TOTAL IN SERVICE	13
CAPACITY	CLUB PREMIERE-28 SEATS
	ECONOMY CLASS-126 SEATS
ENGINES	CFM 56 7B24
CRUISE SPEED	871 KMPH
LENGTH	39.5 METER
WING SPAN	34.3 METER

BOEING 737-700

TOTAL IN SERVICE	11
CAPACITY	CLUB PREMIERE-20
	ECONOMY CLASS-102
ENGINES	CFM 56 7B22
CRUISE SPEED	871 KMPH
LENGTH	33.6 METER
WING SPAN	34.3 METER

BOEING 737-400

TOTAL IN SERVICE	08
CAPACITY	CLUB PREMIERE-24
	ECONOMY CLASS-112
ENGINES	CFM 563C1

CRUISE SPEED	81.5 KMPH
LENGTH	36.4 METER
WIND SPAN	28.9 METER
ATR 72-500	
TOTAL IN SERVICE	08
CAPACITY	ECONOMY CLASS-62
ENGINES	PW127F
CRUISE SPEED	511 KMPH
LENGTH	27.17 METER
WING SPAN	27.0 METER

Source: Field Survey.

APPENDIX–VII

Jet Airways (Cargo)

Flight No.	*Registration No.*	*Series*	*Booked load*	*Cargo planned*
9W-302	JGC	900	24/140	2900 K
9W-922	JNV	700	20/109	1400K
9W-815	JNV	700	16/119	1700K
9W-602	JGA	800	17/128	2800K
9W-829	JNQ	700	05/41	2100K
9W-333	JNS	700	14/102	1800K+Mail
9W-317	JNC	ATR	47	400K
9W-306	JNW	700	07/69	1800K
9W-603	JAR	400	13/115	2100K+Mail
9W-605	JAS	400	07/113	2000K
9W-3303	JGD	ATR	40	4000K
9W-352	JGD	900	12/91	

Day Charges

Sector	*Flight*	*Rate*	*Slab*	*Min charges*
DEL-AHM	9W-705	10:15	+100	1015
DEL-CCU	9W-911	14:70	+100	1420
DEL-HYD	9W-825	16:80	+100	1680

Source: Field Survey.

APPENDIX–VIII

JET AIRWAYS CATERING

Jet Airways Catering Comes from Taj and Oberoi

Different types of meal are as follows:

Meal Plan	*Abbreviations*
DBML	Diabetic Meal
GFML	Glutone Free meal
LSML	Low Sugar Meal
LFML	Low Fat Meal
LCML	Low Calorie Meal
LPML	Low Protein Meal
HFML	High Fiber Meal
BLML	Bland Meal
CHML	Children Meal
VGML	Veg Meal
SPML	Special Meal
NVML	Non-Veg Meal
FPML	Fruit Platter Meal
MOML	Moslem Meal
PLML	Low Purine Meal
LSML	Low Salt Meal
NLML	No Dairy Lactose Free
SFML	Sea Food Meal

Special Meals

Type of Meal	*Choice-I*	*Choice-II*	*Choice-III*
DBML	Fruit compote No syrup Scrambled egg Hash brown, Mushroom	Fruit compote No syrup Veg Bhaji paratha, Chingri matar	Fruit composte No syrup Chana masala Veg bhaji
AVML	Paneer, Bhurji Veg Cutlet Paratha	Idly Coconut chutney Upma	Chole Poori Watana masala

MOML	Scramble egg Grilled tomato mushroom Mushroom	Meeda Omelet Chin, sausage Potato permenter	Paneer bhaji Aaloo paratha Paratha
ULML	Paneer bhurji Veg cutlet Paratha	Idly Coconut chutney Upma	Chole Poori Watan masala
LFML	Egg while omlette Hash brown potato Grilled tomato, mushroom	Poached fish Boiled potato Boiled veg	Baked beans Mushroom Grilled tomato Spinach
LCML	Egg while omlette Hash brown potato Grilled tomato, mushroom	Poached fish Boiled potato Boiled veg Spinach	Baked beans Mushroom Grilled tomato
LPML	Corn filter, Tomato msurhoom Beans in tomato sauce Sweet potato	Poached fish Potato croquette Grilled pepper	Veg Florentine
PRML	Omlette Grilled tomato Hash brown potato Sweet potato	Baked bean in tomato Sauce, grilled pepper Mushroom	Poached chicken Tomato Potato

Source: Field Survey.

APPENDIX–IX

CLASS OF JET AIRWAYS

There are two class of jet airways:

1. Club Premier
2. Economy class

C: USD fare business class

A: INR fare business class

Y: USD fare economy class

M: INR fare economy class

The following categories can avail the concession of 9W

Senior citizen	30%
LTC (for Govt. employee)	50%
Blind	50%
Cancer Patient	50%
Student	50%
Military	50%
Child	50%

Source: Field Survey.

APPENDIX–X

NAME AND ADDRESSES OF THE AIRLINES

Direct Carriers	
Air India Jeevan Bharti Building Connaught Place New Delhi-110 001	British Airways G.S.A. – Nijhawan Travel Services Pvt. Ltd. F-53, Bhagat Singh Market, New Delhi-110 001 Tel: 3365425
European Carriers	
Air France7, Atma Ram Mension Scindia House,Connaught Place New Delhi-110 001Tel.: 3310068	Lufthansa German Airlines 54, Alps Building, Janpath Connaught Place New Delhi-110 001
KLM North West Airlines Prakash Deep Building 7, Tolstoy Marg, New Delhi-110 001 Tel: 3720447	Swiss Air 1st Floor, DLS Centre, Parliament Street, New Delhi-110 001
Australian Airlines 5th Floor, Hindustan Times Building, Kasturba Gandhi Marg, New Delhi-110 001	SAS Ground Floor, Ambadeep Building, Kasturba Gandhi Marg, New Delhi-110 001 Tel: 3352299
Middle East Carriers	
Emirates Kanchanjunga Building 18, Barakhamba Road New Delhi-110 001 Tel: 3324384	Gulf Air 9-11, Cannought circus Connaught Place, New Delhi-110 001 Tel: 3325929
Kuwait Airways 106, Ansal Bhawan	Royal Jordanian G-56, Cannought Circus

16, Kasturba Gandhi Marg New Delhi-110 001 Tel: 3354377	Connaught Place, New Delhi-110 001 Tel: 3721786
CIS Carriers	
Aeroflot – Russian International Airlines Tolstoy House 15-17, Tolstoy Marg, New Delhi-110 001	Air Kazakstan GF-3, Ansal Bhawan 16, Kasturba Gandhi Marg, New Delhi-110 001 Tel: 3352032
Turkmenistan Airlines N-1, BMC House Middle Circle, Connaught Place New Delhi-110 001 Tel: 3721085	Uzbekistan Airways 3, Ground Floor Prakash Deep Building 7 Tostoy Marg, New Delhi-110 001 Tel: 3358687

Source: Field Survey.

APPENDIX-XI

LIST OF SELECTED TRAVEL AGENCIES

S.No.	Category A
01.	American Express Tour40-41, Community Centre, Bhilwara Bhawan,New Friends Colony, New Delhi Tel: 6318722
02.	Balmer Lawrie and Co. Ltd.Lodhi Road, New Delhi.
03.	Cox & KingsIndra Place, H-Block, Connaught Place, New Delhi-110 001Tel: 162609
04.	Nijhawan Travel Services Pvt. Ltd.F-53, Bhagat Singh Market, New Delhi-110 001Tel: 3365425
05.	Sita World Travel Ltd.F-12, Connaught Place, New Delhi-110 001Tel: 3311122
06.	Thomas Cook India Ltd.C-33, Inner Circle Connaught Place, New Delhi-110 001Tel: 3356575
	Category B
07.	Entees78/1, Janpath, 1st Floor, Connaught Place, New Delhi-110 001Tel: 3310066
08.	Orient Express Travel & Tours70, Janpath, Connaught Place, New Delhi-110 001Tel: 3322142
	Category C
09.	President Tours Service811, Arunachal Building, 19, B.K. Road, Connaught PlaceNew Delhi-110 001Tel: 3310797
10.	Shikhar Travels209, Competent House, F-14, Middle Circle, Connaught Place,New Delhi-110 001Tel: 3312444
11.	Vision Travel & Tours1-M, CM Building, Barakhamba Road, Connaught Place,New Delhi-110 001Tel: 3715199

Source: Field Survey.

APPENDIX–XII

ORGANIZATIONAL CHART OF ITDC

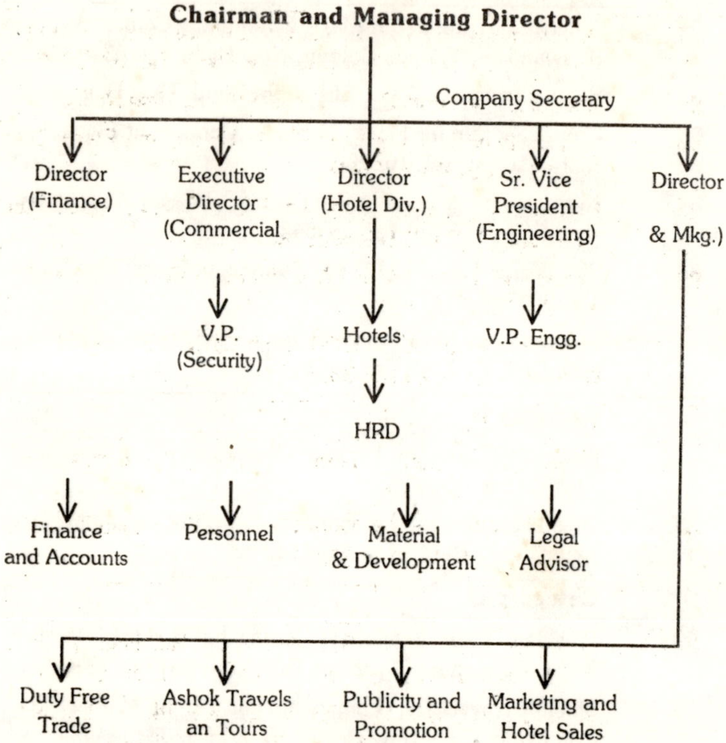

Source: 39th Annual Report (2003-04), India Tourism Development Corporation, Scope Complex, New Delhi, p. 134.

APPENDIX–XIII

THE NETWORK OF ITDC SERVICES

Accommodation (The Ashok Group)

A. HOTELS

1. Ashok Hotel, New Delhi
2. Hotel Janpath, New Delhi
3. Hotel Jammu Ashok, Jammu
4. Lalitha Mahal Palace Hotel, Mysore
5. Hotel Pataliputra Ashok, Patna
6. Hotel Jaipur Ashok, Jaipur
7. Hotel Kalinga Ashok, Bhubaneswar
8. Hotel Samrat, New Delhi

Ashok Restaurants

1. Taj Restaurant, Agra
2. Airport Restaurant, Delhi

Travel / Transport Unit

1 Varanasi
2. Bangalore
3. Chennai
4. Aurangabad
5. Patna
6. Delhi
7. Kolkata
8. Mumbai
9. Ranchi
10. Guwahati
11. Jaipur
12. Hyderabad

Tourist Service Station
Chanakyapuri, New Delhi

Duty Free Shops

Location	No. of Shop
1. Delhi Airport Dep. Lounge	8
2. Delhi Airport Dep. Lounge	2
3. Kolkata Airport Dep. Lounge	1
4. Kolkata Airport Arr. Lounge	3

5.	Mumbai Airport Dep. Lounge	8
6.	Mumbai Airport Arr. Lounge	3
7.	Chennai Airport Dep. Lounge	1
8.	Chennai Airport Arr. Lounge	1
9.	Trivandrum Airport Dep. Lounge	1
10.	Trivandrum Airport Arr. Lounge	1
11.	Gia Airport Arr. Lounge	1
12.	Goa Airport Dept. Lounge	1
13.	Calicut Airport Arr. Lounge	1
14.	Calicut Airport Dep. Lounge	1
15.	Bangalore Airport Dept. Lounge	1
16.	Bangalore Airport Arr. Lounge	1
17.	Hyderabad Airport Dep. Lounge	1
18.	Hyderabad Airport Arr. Lounge	1
19.	Ahmedabad Airport Dep. Lounge	1
20.	Ahmedabad Airport Arr. Lounge	1
	Total	37

Sound & Light Shows

1. Red Fort, Delhi
2. Sabarmati Ashram, Ahmedabad

B. JOINT VENTURE HOTELS

1. Hotel Brahmaputra Ashok, Guwahati
2. Hotel Ranchi Ashok, Ranchi
3. Hotel Nilachal Ashok, Puri
4. Hotel Pondicherry Ashok, Pondicherry
5. Hotel Lake View Ashok, Bhopal
6. Hotel Donyi Polo Ashok, Itanagar
7. Hotel Anandpur Sahib, Anandpur (under construction)

C. MANAGED UNITS

Hotel

Hotel Bharatpur Ashok, Bharatpur

Restaurant

Kosi Restaurant, Kosi

Catering Establishments

1. State Guest House & Hospitality Centre at Hyderabad House, New Delhi
2. Western Court Catering Service, New Delhi
3. Ashok Mayur Restaurant, Vigyan Bhawan, New Delhi
4. Media Press Centre, Shastri Bhavan, New Delhi

Source: 39th Annual Report (2003-04), India Tourism Development Corporation, Scope Complex, New Delhi, p. 17.

APPENDIX -XIV

APPLICATION FORMAT FOR RECRUITMENT IN ITDC

Application for the post of:

1. Full Name (in Block Letters):
2. Father's Name and Occupation:
3. Permanent Home Address:
4. Present Postal Address:
5. Nationality:
   (State whether by birth or domicile:
6. Date of Birth (Age):
7. Sex (Male/Female):
8. Category: SC/ST/OBC:
9. Religion
10. Educational/Professional Qualification:

Affix passport size photograph

Sl. No.	Examination Passed	Name of the Subject details	Year of passing	Percentage of marks	School/Board/ University

11. Experience including present occupation

Sl. No.	Name of Employer(s) and Designation	Period of Service From To	Length of Service	Total salary per month drawn	Nature of Duties

12. Indicate three options of placement out of: Jaipur/Agra/Patna/ Bhubaneshwar/Guwahati/Bhopal
13. Any other Information:

I hereby declare that I fulfil the eligibility conditions as per the advertisement and that all the statements made in this application are true, complete and correct to the best of my knowledge and belief. I understand that in the event of any information being found false or incorrect at any stage or not satisfying the eligibility conditions according to the requirements mentioned in the advertisement, my candidature/appointment is liable to be cancelled/ terminated.

Place:

Dated: **Signature**

Source: **www.theashokgroup.com**

BOOKS

Agarwal, R.D., (2001), *Dynamics of Personnel Management in India,* Tata McGraw Hill Publishing Co., New Delhi.

Agarwal, S.P., (2004), *Manpower Supply: Concepts and Methodology,* Meenakshi Prakashan, Meerut.

Arthur, A. Thomson and A.J. Strickland, (2003), *Strategic Management,* McGraw Hill, New York.

Aswathappa, K., (2005), *Human Resource and Personnel Management – Text and Cases,* Tata McGraw Hill Publishing Company Ltd., New Delhi.

Bartholomew, J.J. and Morris, B.R., (1971), *Aspects of Manpower Planning,* The English Universities Press, London.

Bass, Barnard M. and Vaughan, J.A., (1998), *Training in Industries: The Management of Learning,* Wordsworth Publishing Co., California Belmont.

Basu, K.S., (1998), *New Dimensions in Personnel Management,* Macmillan & Co., New Delhi.

Batra, G.S. and Chawla, A.S., (2001), *Tourism Management – A Global Perspective,* Deep and Deep Publications Pvt. Ltd., New Delhi.

Batra, G.S. and Dangwal, R.C., (2001), *Tourism Promotion and Development–New Advances,* Deep and Deep Publications Pvt. Ltd., New Delhi.

Bhasin, M.L., (2004), *Human Resource Management–The Case Studies,* Anmol Publications, New Delhi.

Datt, Mridula Narayan (2004), *Ecology and Tourism,* Universal Publishers, Distributors, Delhi.

Davar, Rustom, S., (2002), *Personnel Management and Industrial Relations in India,* Vikas Publishing House Pvt. Ltd., New Delhi.

Dessler, Garry, (2005), *Human Resource Management,* Prentice-Hall of India Pvt. Ltd., New Delhi.

Eli Ginzberg and Smith, H.A., (1967), *Manpower Strategy for Developed Countries,* Columbia University Press.

Feldman and Arnold, (1983), *Managing Individual and Group Behaviour in Organisations,* McGraw Hill, New York.

Finbli, Robert B. and Jones, William S., (2001), *Assessing Corporate Talent – A Key to Managerial Manpower Planning,* John Wiley & Sons Inc., U.S.A.

Flippo, Edwin, B., (2002), *Personnel Management,* McGraw Hill Book Company, New York.

Ghosh, P., (2002), *Personnel Administration in India,* Sudha Publications Pvt. Ltd., New Delhi.

Ginsberg, Eli, (1999), *The Development of Human Resources,* McGraw Hill, New York.

Gordon, R.A., (2000), *Towards a Manpower Policy,* John Wiley & Sons Inc., New York.

Gupta, C.B., (2003), *Human Resource Management,* Sultan Chand & Sons, New Delhi.

Gupta, Sunil and Bansal, S.P. (2001), *Tourism Towards 21st Century,* Deep & Deep Publication Pvt. Ltd., New Delhi.

Gvin, Robert, M., (1995), *Personnel Training,* McGraw Hill, New York.

Harbison, F. and Charles, A. Myers, (1995), *Education, Manpower and Economic Growth,* McGraw Hill, New York.

Harris, O., Jeff, Jr. (2002), *Managing People at Work: Concepts and Cases in Inter-Personal Behaviour,* John Wiley & Sons, New York.

Hax, Arnold C., (2001), *Planning Strategies that Work,* Oxford University Press, New York.

Henderson, Richard L., *Compensation Management,* Reston Publishing House, New York.

John, F. Hilliard, (2001), *Dynamics of Development,* Universal Book Stall, Delhi.

John, M. Ivancevich, (2004), *Human Resource Management,* Tata McGraw Hill, New York.

John, H. Bernardian and Joyce, E.A. Russell, (1999), *Human Resource Management–An Experimental Approach,* McGraw Hill, New York.

Kamra, Krishan K., (2002), *Basics of Tourism – Theory, Operation and Practice,* Kanishka, New Delhi.

Kandula, Srinivas R., (2004), *Strategic Human Resource Development,* Prentice-Hall of India Private Limited, New Delhi.

Khan, Nafees A. (2008), *HRD in Tourism Industry,* Zenith Books International Delhi.

Kumar, Ashok, (2004), *Human Resource Management: Challenge of Change*, Anmol Publications Pvt. Limited, New Delhi.

Lallan, Prasad and Banerjee, A.M., (2005), *Management of Human Resources*, Sterling Publishers Pvt. Ltd., New Delhi.

Lester, R.A., (1966), *Manpower Planning in a Free Society*, Princeton University Press.

Luis, R. Gomez and Mejia, et al. (2003), *Managing Human Resources*, Prentice Hall of India, New Delhi.

MacFarland, D.E., (2001), *Personnel Management: Theory and Practice*, Macmillan & Co., New York.

Megginson, L.C., (1991), *Human Resources, Cases and Concepts*, Harcourt Brace, Ivancevich.

Mamoria, C.B. and Gankar, S.V., (2002), *Personnel Management*, Himalaya Publishing House, Mumbai.

Michael, R. Carrell, et al. (1992), *Personnel/Human Resource Management*, Maxwell Macmillan.

Milkovich and Boudreau, (1990), *Personnel – Human Resource Management*, Richard D. Irwin.

Monappa, Arun, and Saiyadain, Mirza, (2002), *Personnel Management*, Tata McGraw Hill Publishing Co. Ltd., New Delhi.

Pattanayak, Biswajeet, (2004), *Human Resource Management*, Prentice Hall of India Pvt. Ltd., New Delhi.

Patten, T.H., (2000), *Manpower Planning and Development of Human Resources*, Wiley, New York.

Raina, Chaman Lal and Rain, Abhinav, K., (2005), *Fundamentals of Tourism and Indian Religions – Principles and Practices*, Kanishka, New Delhi.

Randall, S. Schuler, (1996), *Personnel and Human Resource Management*, West Publishing Co. St. Paul.

Rao, V.K.R.V., (2003), *Education and Human Resource Development*, Allied Publishers, Bombay.

Raymond Noe, et al. (2000), *Human Resource Management*, Irwin McGraw Hill.

Robbins, Stephens, P., (2003), *Personnel: The Management of Human Resources*, Prentice-Hall of India, New Delhi.

Rudrabasavaraj, M.N., (2002), *Dynamic Personnel Administration – Management of Human Resources*, Himalaya Publishing House, Bombay.

Sabhanayakam, S. (2002), *Human Resources: Development and Utilization (with special reference to India)*, Renaissance Publishing House, Delhi.

Sarkar, Arun Kumar and Dhar, Premnath, (2004), *Indian Tourism – Economic Planning and Strategies,* Kanishka, New Delhi.

Sarma, A.M., (2003), *Personnel and Human Resource Management,* Himalaya Publishing House, Mumbai.

Sen, A.K., (2004), *Economic Approaches to Education and Manpower Planning,* Asian Institute for Economic Development and Planning, Bangkok.

Seth, Pran Nath and Bhat, Sushma, (2002), *An Introduction to Travel and Tourism,* Sterling Publishers Pvt. Ltd., New Delhi.

Sharma, K.C., (2003), *Tourism: Policy, Planning and Strategy,* Pointer Publishers, Jaipur.

Singh, Percy K., (2003), *Fifty Years of Indian Tourism,* Kanishka, New Delhi.

Singh, Ratandeep, (2003), *Dynamics of Modern Tourism,* Kanishka, New Delhi.

Singh, Ratandeep, (2003), *Infrastructure of Tourism in India,* Kanishka, New Delhi.

Stainer, G., (1971), *Manpower Planning: The Management of Human Resources,* Heinann, London.

Tripathi, P.C., (2005), *Human Resource Development,* Sultan Chand & Sons, New Delhi.

Venkataratnam, C.S. and Srivastava, B.K., (2005), *Personnel Management and Human Resources,* Tata McGraw Hill Publishing Co., New Delhi.

Walley, B.H. (2001), *Management Services Handbook,* Business Books Limited, London.

Wasmuth, W.J., Simong, R.H., Hilgert, R.L., and Lee, H.C. (2000), *Human Resources Administration: Problems of Growth and Change,* Boston, Houghton Mifflin & Co., Boston.

Wayne, F. (1995), *Managing Human Resources,* McGraw Hill, New York.

Wayne, Mondey R. and Robert, M. Noe III (2001), *Personnel – The Management of Human Resources,* Allyn & Bacon, Boston.

William, W. Werther Jr. and Keith, Davis, (1993), *Human Resources and Personnel Management,* Fourth Edition, McGraw Hill, New York.

William, J. Rothwell, (2002), *Strategic Human Resource Planning and Management,* Prentice Hall, New Delhi.

REPORTS

Annual Report (2006-07), India Tourism, Government of India, New Delhi.

Tourist Statistics (2006-07), W.T.O., Madrid.

Thirty-Ninth Annual Report (2006-07), ITDC, New Delhi

Annual Report (2006-07), Ministry of Civil Aviation, Government of India, New Delhi.

Annual Report (2006-07), Indian Institute of Tourism and Travel Management, Gwalior.

Report, National Committee on Tourism (1988), Planning Commission, Government of India, New Delhi.

JOURNALS/PERIODICALS/MAGAZINES

- *Indrama*, Oct-Dec. 2005.
- *International Journal of Tourism and Management* (1993), Jodhpur, India.
- *International Journal of Tourism Research* (2004), Scotland.
- *Journal of Annals of Tourism Research*, Vol. VII(1), 2004.
- *Kurukshetra* (June-Nov., 2004), Krishi Bhawan, New Delhi.
- *Prabandh* (Oct.-June 2004), Bureau of State Enterprises, Lucknow.
- *Tourism and Wild Life* (2004), New Delhi.
- *Tourism Development Journal*, Vol. 1, No. 1, 2003, Shimala, Himachal Pradesh.
- *Tourism Recreation Research* (July-Dec., 2004), Lucknow.
- *Travel Links*, Feb.-July, 2005.
- *Yojana*, (July-Oct., 2005), Yojana Bhawan, New Delhi.

WEBSITES

www.indiatourism.com

www.itdc.org

www.tourismofindia.com

www.travelindia.com

Index

A

Adventure tourism, 53
Air Sahara, 17, 117, 118, 132, 150
  special services, 119-135
Airlines in India, 158
Ancillary industries, 41
APETIT, 24
Art and crafts, 50
Asia, private airlines in, 158
Aswathappa, K, 20
Aviation, 33

B

Bhasin ML, 21
Bhatia, AK, 27
Bhatnagar, KP, 25
British Airways, 119

C

Coleman, 64
Cost control, 75

D

Davar, Rustom S, 22
Dessler, Garry, 19
Duty free shops, 139

E

Ecotourism, 50

F

Fairs and festivals, 51
Finble, RB, 23
Flippo, Edwin B, 21
Folk music and dance, 51

G

Government of India, 60
Gupta, CB, 23

H

Hax, Anoldo C, 23
Hospitality education sectior, 104
Hotel' the Park', 84-94, 95
  rectuitment process in, 37
HRIS, 69
  need of, 70
Human Capital, 7, 8
Human resource 1
  development of, 2
  role of planning of, 3
  vs. human capital, 8
Human Resource Planning, 2, 3, 19, 30
  dimensions of, 67
  need for, 78
  problems and issues, 12-14
  strategies, 5-6
  significance of, 74

systematic, 6
theoretical perspective, 61-80

I

IGNOU, 103
IITM, 44
ILO, 24
ITDC, 17, 18, 32, 43, 117, 137-148, 156, 157, 173, 177
accommodation chain of, 137
Board of Directors, 138
disinvestments in, 142
HRM in, 138
organisation setup, 138

J

Jainism, 49
Jet Airways, 17, 117, 125, 151
merger, 131
services, offered by, 124-134
Jet Airways, 17

K

Kandula, Srinivas R. 19
Kautilya, 12
Kumar, Ashok, 20

L

Labour Management, 11
Ladakh, 56
London, 42

M

Malhotra, RK, 26
Mamoria, CB, 21
Manpower Plan, 76
objectives, 77
tools and techniques, 77
Mathur, Navin, 28
Matiram, 26
Monappa, Arun, 20
Maintaineering, 45

N

Narayan, B, 28
Narayanrao, 14
National Committee on Tourism, 24
National Institute of Personnel Management of India, 24
NCHMCT, 103
National Parks and sanctuaries, 52
New York, 42

P

Painting, 50
Personnel Management, 11
Placement, 83
Planning Commission, 46, 66
Prasad, LM, 25
Prasad, VRK, 25

R

Recruitment, 81
and selection, 81-94
River Rafting, 154
Rudrabasavaraj, MN, 22

S

Scott, WG, 27
Selection, 82, 83
Society for Human Resource Management (SHRM), 10
Stainer, 5, 64
Stainer, 64
Suri, G.K., 10

T

TDP, 99
Tourism Sector (India), 30-60

adventure, 53-55
cultural, 50
aspect, 41
economic aspect, 34
employment aspect, 35
foreign exchange earning from, 30
forms and products of, 47
heritage, 55
planned development, 42, 47
publicity, 35
religious, 48
significance of, 31
social perspective, 39
Tourist arrivals, 36
TQM, 101
Training and development, 95-116
difference between, 97
methods of, 100
programmes in tourism, 102
objectives, 98
Trekking, 53
Tripathy, PC, 19

U

UNEP, 24
United Nations, 8
United States, 10

V

Valley of Flowers, 53
Velter, 65

W

Walley, BH, 23
Water sports, 55
Wickstrom, 64
WTO, 24
WTTC, 24

Y

Yoder, Dale, 21